REASON AND REVELATION

*Scholarly Writings about
The Urantia Book*

General Editor:

Byron Belitsos

Origin Press / Academic

Origin Press / Academic
www.OriginPress.org
Copyright © 2024 by Byron Belitsos

Front cover design by Derek Samaras

ISBN 978-1-57983-065-6 (paperback)
ISBN 978-1-57983-066-3 (ebook)

Printed in the United States of America

Contents

Editor's Preface

This anthology aims to provide, in one introductory volume, the highest quality research essays about *The Urantia Book*, a dense text of 2,097 pages that is also known as the *UB*, Urantia revelation, Urantia text, or *Urantia Papers*. The *UB* is described by adherents as an "epochal" revelation to humankind and is felt by many to be a new "bible" for the postmodern world. Upon inspection, the *UB* comes across as a futuristic encyclopedia of theology, modern cosmology, science, spirituality, religion, philosophy, and history. One also discovers that 775 of its pages provide an audacious retelling of the life and teachings of Jesus, purportedly based on the angelic and human record of these events and intended to update or correct the errors of the New Testament. *The Urantia Book* was first published in 1955 in Chicago, the city where the manuscript originated through a "contact commission" of six individuals (as described in chapter 5). This group was led by a surgeon and psychiatrist named Dr. William Sadler, who studied with Sigmund Freud in Vienna for a year in 1910 and who later authored *Theory and Practice of Psychiatry* (1936), among numerous popular and professional books. Sadler and his supporters founded the Urantia Foundation, which today claims sales of over one million copies in more than 20 languages and a large following worldwide.

The pieces in this anthology were chosen because they showcase genuine scholarship or in-depth research. These essays were also selected because they are suited for readers who are new to the *UB* and in most cases provide such inquirers with a helpful bridge to contemporary knowledge outside the Urantia text. It is our further intention that this anthology may inspire scholarly publications that serve as valid contributions to religious studies, philosophy, theology, history, general humanities, or for classroom use in these fields of study.

One may well hope for such a salutary result, but as I write this in early 2024, the publication of scholarly works in venues not solely intended for the Urantia reader-believer community (as we call it) are very rare. In the decades since the book was first published in 1955, such an endeavor has been perilous for academics and professional researchers. As you read these essays, you'll discover why; because of its claim to be revelatory information of epochal significance, *The Urantia Book* is regarded as transgressive—especially by mainstream scholars.

And it is for this reason that three of our most significant contributors chose to use pseudonyms. In fact, almost all deep students of this purported epochal revelation prefer to write for the wider community of *UB* students, thus avoiding controversy and rejection. *Reason and Revelation* is an early effort to put an end to this sharp division between the little-known Urantia community and the wider intelligentsia of today's society.

Like the *Urantia Book* teachings themselves, this anthology is holistic and interdisciplinary. However, it does not provide essays covering the social and natural sciences, which will be collected in a future volume.

Reason and Revelation is divided into four parts:

I. General Studies
II. Origin and Influence Studies
III. Religion, Ethics, and Spirituality
IV. Philosophy and Theology

Because no prior knowledge of the *UB* is required, Part I provides a beginner's orientation, as does the Introduction that follows this Preface. This preliminary material provides a general overview and should be considered required reading for those new to the Urantia text. For more advanced definitions and explanations of key concepts, readers can go to specific essays in Parts II, III, or IV or turn to the glossary.

Please note also that each part begins with a Prologue that features epigrammatic *UB* quotes pertinent to that section.

Most but not all of the later essays in this anthology are chosen because they are comparative, that is, they assess the *UB*'s teachings in relation to the contemporary academic understanding of the chosen topic. Chapters 9, 10, and 11 were chosen especially because they showcase advanced studies of important topics written by professional academics, two of whom are anonymous; it is our hope that these essays will inspire readers to look up and study their many citations. And finally, to further aid readers, *Reason and Revelation* provides appendices and an extensive glossary, which covers the many words and phrases unique to the Urantia revelation.

A Beginner's Overview of the Parts of *The Urantia Book*

Claimed by its authors to be an "epochal" revelation, the *UB* comes across at first glance as a futuristic encyclopedia of theology, cosmology, spirituality, science, religion, philosophy, and history. Upon deeper inspection, one discovers something startling: 775 of its 2,097 pages recount the life and teachings of Jesus, purportedly based on the angelic record of these events as well as on human records.[1] This unprecedented narrative comprises the last of the book's four sections.

Other large sections describe the *local universe* of over six million inhabited planets and the five-billion-year story of our planet, whose

---

[1] This approach to the compilation is explained by the revelators: "As far as possible, consistent with our mandate, we have endeavored to utilize and to some extent co-ordinate the existing records having to do with the life of Jesus on Urantia. Although *we have enjoyed access to the lost record of the Apostle Andrew and have benefited from the collaboration of a vast host of celestial beings who were on earth during the times of [the life of Jesus], it has been our purpose also to make use of the so-called Gospels of Matthew, Mark, Luke, and John. . . .*The memoranda which I have collected, and from which I have prepared this narrative of the life and teachings of Jesus—aside from the memory of the record of the Apostle Andrew—embrace thought gems and superior concepts of Jesus' teachings assembled from more than two thousand human beings who have lived on earth from the days of Jesus down to the time of the inditing of these revelations, more correctly restatements. The revelatory permission has been utilized only when the human record and human concepts failed to supply an adequate thought pattern. My revelatory commission forbade me to resort to extrahuman sources of either information or expression until such a time as I could testify that I had failed in my efforts to find the required conceptual expression in purely human sources" (121:8). [Emphasis added.]

"universe name" is said to be *Urantia*. All of this is framed very broadly by Part I, which provides a theology, philosophy, and multidimensional map of the cosmos that we believe is commensurate with our age of quantum physics, artificial intelligence, evolutionary biology, and multiverse cosmology.

Following is an overview of the anatomy and contents of *The Urantia Book*, which features a lengthy Foreword plus 196 "Papers" (or chapters) and is divided into four large parts.

Part I. "The Central and Superuniverses" presents the infinitely loving and merciful nature of the Universal Father, the "First Source and Center" of all things and beings whose attributes are utterly beyond gender. It also depicts his absolute and coordinate deity equals—the Eternal Son and the Infinite Spirit—as well as the self-distributions of the Trinity into all domains of reality.

The three eternal Persons are distinct "source-personalities" with differing attributes, but they can act as one perfectly unified Trinity and may also function in various permutations for diverse purposes. This section further depicts the universe activities associated with the "reality domains" of each of member of the Trinity, plus the nature and functions of the high universe personalities created by them—while offering still other disclosures about the ultimate nature of deity, divinity, and the cosmos including the so-called "Seven Absolutes of Infinity" (which embraces all personal and impersonal realities in all universes).

Part I also describes the far-flung domains of universal creation, painting a riveting picture of the perfect, eternal, and extra-dimensional central universe that lies at the center of the evolving time-space universe and that serves as its infinite source. At the very core of this eternal mother universe is *Paradise*, the everlasting residence of the Persons of the Trinity as well the home of a unique population of perfect citizens, its permanent inhabitants. The *Isle of Paradise*, as it is often called, is also the longed-for destiny of all ascending pilgrims hailing from the lowly material planets. Paradise is the motionless center-point of infinity and the absolute paragon, pattern, and source of all forms of energy, gravity, and matter in all domains and dimensions. Entirely surrounding the central universe is a region called *Havona*—which contains the highest-dimension spheres, worlds that exist from eternity and are populated by "non-experiential" perfect citizens. The central universe is, again, extra-dimensional and is therefore invisible to those looking inward toward it from the time-space domains. Encircling Havona is a stupendous ring of material galaxies containing inhabited planets and comprising the *grand universe* (as noted). And beyond this are four regions of organized creation containing trillions of uninhabited galaxies called "the outer space levels," now coming into better visibility thanks to the James Webb Space Telescope. I believe there is nothing in world literature comparable to the lofty exposition of the cosmic and theological realities depicted in Part I, or the complex overview provided in the Foreword.

Part II. "The Local Universe" details the origin, nature, and structure of the "local" sector of our Milky Way galaxy that contains about six million inhabited planets, also covering its history, administration, and governance. The organization of a local universe features many subdivisions down to the level of *local systems* that encompass up to 1,000 inhabited worlds. In addition, this section details the vast celestial (or angelic) host of the local creation who, as mentioned earlier, ministers in co-creative fashion to the human inhabitants on each material planet and also provides for the implantation and overcontrol of all forms of evolving life.

Part II offers considerable detail on the *ascension scheme*, the divine plan for each person's afterlife ascent toward ultimate perfection that proceeds in a long series of "graduations" upwards through increasingly more rarefied worlds. The final stop in the local universe is the glorious headquarters sphere called *Salvington*, the last step before entering the more advanced *superuniverse* regime of ascent that leads upward and inward to the central universe and then to Paradise.

All pilgrims from our planet will awake after death on what is known as the *first mansion world*—the very first of the abodes of heavenly life. (Cf. John 14:2: "In my Father's house are many mansions.")

Each ascender begins their afterlife career on that world, embarking on a vast regime of self-understanding, personal healing, spiritual training, holistic education, and cosmic socialization (a process whose full description is spread across Parts I–III in the text.)

One of the highlights of Part II is the introduction of the Father-Creator of our local universe known as *Christ Michael*. It is he who incarnated as Jesus of Nazareth on Urantia. Also introduced is Michael's complemental deity partner and perfectly coequal Co-Creator (with him) of this local universe, the *Universe Mother Spirit*. They both reside on Salvington as our compassionate Creators and local-universe rulers.

Part III. "The History of Urantia" narrates the astrophysical origin of our solar system and offers a chronological account of the entire history of earth (Urantia) beginning with the implantation and evolution of all life on the planet, and including the biological, anthropological, racial, and spiritual history of humankind. This section also unveils and unpacks the story of the four previous epochal revelations to Urantia—*The Urantia Book* being the fifth.

Significantly, Part III includes detail about the *Lucifer Rebellion* that traumatized Urantia as well as 36 other planets in the local system. This event occurred in the far-distant past but its effects are still profoundly felt. This rare disaster of planet-wide angelic rebellion led to the default and wreckage of the first two phases of epochal revelation on our sphere.[2] This gloomy start to humankind's history was the key reason why Christ Michael chose to incarnate on our lowly sphere as Jesus of Nazareth. We are told that Urantia's disastrous history— its unique burden of sin and suffering—offered the starkest backdrop against which to demonstrate Michael's sublime and merciful love for his most wayward human creatures.

Part III then provides a comprehensive picture of the seven-stage process known as "cosmic individuation." This complex but coherent discussion details the nature and function of the soul and the

---

[2] These epochal visitations include the earth mission of Adam and Eve, one of the most dramatic and fascinating narratives in the Urantia text.

phenomenon of soul evolution before and after death; the true nature and function of religion; the nature of personhood as well as the concept of the *Indwelling Spirit*, also called the Father Fragment, that is dispatched to live within the minds of each one of us to guide us to perfection. This entity of pure divinity works in tandem with our powers of choice to co-create our soul as we engage in the work of soul-making.

Whereas Part I introduced the Eternal Trinity on Paradise, Part III reveals the evolving cosmic deity known as the *Supreme Being*, the dynamic repository and synthesis of the totality of ongoing creator-Creator experience in the grand universe.

Part IV. "The Life and Teachings of Jesus" contains a comprehensive account of Jesus's life, in actuality a coherent "restatement" based on human, biblical, and angelic sources. This expansive narrative often covers events day by day and sometimes hour by hour—including the story of the "lost years" of Jesus's childhood, adolescence, and young adulthood. It also contains an extensive account of his private and public ministries, his miracles, and his wide proclamation of the Gospel in the form of personal instruction, parables, sermons, and interactions with the Apostles and close disciples.

In its 180-page closing section, Part IV details the last week of his life, his death and resurrection (and nineteen post-resurrection appearances), and ends with the story of the bestowal of his *Spirit of Truth* at Pentecost. Perhaps the most inspirational material is its culminating paper, "The Faith of Jesus," a "summa" of Jesus's life and message.

Ultimately, readers of Part IV are able to uplift and renew their understanding of Jesus, thanks to a seamless narrative that builds both upon the sacred foundation of the biblical record along with numerous previously unknown episodes. They also discover an elevated portrayal of a Jesus who teaches a Gospel of loving service, self-respect, soul evolution, artistic living, love for one's enemies, self-mastery, and sublime worship of the God on Paradise in the context of the *UB*'s advocacy for planetary and cosmic citizenship.

In regard to its relationship to Christianity, it may be little wonder that some regard the *UB* as a postmodern Bible, but it is more appropriate to say that it provides a very wide range of vital corrections and updates to key biblical narratives and Christian tenets, now transplanted into a modern evolutionary framework and a post-Einstein cosmology.

PART I

GENERAL STUDIES

Prologue I: Excerpts on Epochal Revelation

66 And when the kingdom shall have come to its full fruition, be assured that the Father in heaven will not fail to visit you with an enlarged revelation of truth and an enhanced demonstration of righteousness. 99 *Jesus to the apostles on Mt. Olivet* (176:2.3)

---

66 Revelation is a technique whereby ages upon ages of time are saved in the necessary work of sorting and sifting the errors of evolution from the truths of spirit acquirement. 99 (101:5.1)

---

66 *The Urantia Papers.* The papers, of which this is one, constitute the most recent presentation of truth to the mortals of Urantia. These papers differ from all previous revelations, for they are not the work of a single universe personality but a composite presentation by many beings. But no revelation short of the attainment of the Universal Father can ever be complete. All other celestial ministrations are no more than partial, transient, and practically adapted to local conditions in time and space. While such admissions as this may possibly detract from the immediate force and authority of all revelations, the time has arrived on Urantia when it is advisable to make such frank statements, even at the risk of weakening the future influence and authority of this, the most recent of the revelations of truth to the mortal races of Urantia. 99 (92:4.9)

❝❝ Revelation is evolutionary but always progressive. Down through the ages of a world's history, the revelations of religion are ever-expanding and successively more enlightening. It is the mission of revelation to sort and censor the successive religions of evolution. But if revelation is to exalt and upstep the religions of evolution, then must such divine visitations portray teachings which are not too far removed from the thought and reactions of the age in which they are presented. Thus must and does revelation always keep in touch with evolution. Always must the religion of revelation be limited by man's capacity of receptivity. ❞❞   (92:4.1)

❝❝ The time is ripe to witness the figurative resurrection of the human Jesus from his burial tomb amidst the theological traditions and the religious dogmas of nineteen centuries. Jesus of Nazareth must not be longer sacrificed to even the splendid concept of the glorified Christ. What a transcendent service if, through this revelation, the Son of Man should be recovered from the tomb of traditional theology and be presented as the living Jesus to the church that bears his name, and to all other religions! Surely the Christian fellowship of believers will not hesitate to make such adjustments of faith and of practices of living as will enable it to "follow after" the Master in the demonstration of his real life of religious devotion to the doing of his Father's will and of consecration to the unselfish service of man. . . . Indeed, the social readjustments, the economic transformations, the moral rejuvenations, and the religious revisions of Christian civilization would be drastic and revolutionary if the living religion of Jesus should suddenly supplant the theologic religion about Jesus. ❞❞   (196:1.2)

1

A Pioneer's Early Discovery of *The Urantia Book*

Rev. Dr. Meredith J. Sprunger

Our first two pieces were written by the most influential early advocate for The Urantia Book *outside of the inner circle that received the original papers.*

Meredith Sprunger became the first influential Christian pastor and academic to embrace the Urantia Revelation, discovering it soon after it was published in 1955. He attend a Christian seminary and served in the role of a United Church of Christ pastor with a congregation, later earning a masters in theology from Princeton Theological Seminary and doctorate in psychology from Purdue University. In addition he led a distinguished career as a college professor and later as president of Indiana Technical University. Dr. Sprunger was personally acquainted with three of the six individuals who made up the Contact Commission, the original group that interfaced with the revelators in the compiling of *The Urantia Book* (see chapter 5). Sprunger wrote extensively on topics related to the spread of *The Urantia Book* into the Christian church and on many other topics related to the revelation. Below we provide the story of how he discovered the *UB* in 1955, followed by a sample of one of his many essays introducing the text.

Rev. Dr. Meredith J. Sprunger

My life has been shaped by a series of peak experiences that led me through academic majors in philosophy and theology preparatory to ordination as a minister in the United Church of Christ.

After years of developing sermons and papers formulating my own spiritual experience that was centered in the religion *of* Jesus rather than the religion *about* Jesus, I realized that a new spiritual approach was needed in mainline Christian theology. I tentatively outlined a couple of books that needed to be written, and after some procrastination, I finally committed myself to the discipline of writing these books. Shortly after making this decision, *The Urantia Book* was placed in my hands.

In December of 1955 my wife Irene and I had stopped in to visit our friends, Dr. and Mrs. Edward Brueseke, who resided in South Bend, Indiana. In addition to his pastoral activities, Ed served as chairman of a theological commission in the Evangelical and Reformed Church (which later united with the Congregational Christian denomination to become the United Church of Christ). During the course of the visit Ed picked up a big blue book and handed it to me, saying, "Judge Louis Hammerschmidt (a member of his congregation) gave me this book. Some businessmen think this is a new Bible."

I looked at the table of contents and read chapter headings like "The Messenger Hosts of Space," written by One High in Authority, and "The Corps of the Finality," authored by a Divine Counselor! As I handed the book back to Ed, we had a hearty laugh about businessmen thinking they had a new Bible. I assumed that that would be the last I would see of the book.

At the time I was vice-president of the Indiana-Michigan Conference and Judge Hammerschmidt was the layperson on our conference board. In January I picked up the judge to attend a board meeting in Jackson, Michigan. During the trip Hammerschmidt brought up the topic of spiritualism, which he did not accept, and was a bit surprised that I had made a study of it. After a pause he turned to me and said, "Say, I've got a book that I would like to have you read and tell me what you think of it." I knew he was referring to *The Urantia Book*, but to avoid hurting his feelings I replied, "Okay, Judge. Send it to me."

When the book arrived I set it aside, not wanting to waste my time reading what appeared to be either esoteric nonsense or some elaborate system of theosophy. Periodically, I would read a bit in it here and there but I was not impressed. That summer I took it along on vacation but things didn't get boring enough for me to look at the book. In September I realized that I would be in a meeting with Hammerschmidt in October and I had to read something and tell him what I thought about it.

Looking over the table of contents, I saw it had a section on the life and teachings of Jesus. I thought that with my theological training I could make short work of this section. As I started reading I did not find what I'd expected to find—something like *The Aquarian Gospel of Jesus the Christ*, by Levi. The *Urantia Book*'s story of the early life of Jesus was more believable than the accounts one finds in the apocryphal stories of the boyhood of Jesus. It was, I thought, something that might reasonably have happened.

As I proceeded to read the aspects of the life of Jesus covered by the New Testament I was even more impressed. I discovered that some of the traditional theological problems were handled by the events of the story in a way that made more sense than anything I had ever read.

I found *The Urantia Book*'s narrative to be solidly rooted in the New Testament realities. There were times when I read with tears streaming down my face. When I finished reading "The Life and Teachings of Jesus" I was theologically and spiritually inspired. Whoever had produced a life of Jesus of this quality, I thought, must have something significant to say in the rest of the book.

Thus motivated, I started with the Foreword and read the entire book. I discovered that the first three quarters of the book was even more amazing and profound than "The Life and Teachings of Jesus"! The teachings of *The Urantia Book* resonated and harmonized with my experience and highest thinking. In fact, the substance of the two books I had planned to write was expressed far better here than I could have possibly done. If this is not an authentic picture of spiritual reality, I said to myself, it is the way it ought to be! Science, philosophy, and religion were integrated more effectively in *The Urantia Book* than in any other philosophical or theological system known to me. There was no doubt in my mind that this was the most inspiring and authentic picture of spiritual reality available to humankind.

I gave copies of *The Urantia Book* to around a dozen of my colleagues and all of them except one—who admitted that he hadn't read it—confirmed my evaluation of its high quality. Our clergy group thereupon spent several years interviewing the people connected with the publication of the book and researching events associated with its origin. Since then I have devoted myself to sharing *The Urantia Book* with college students and the clergy of mainline Christianity.

2

A Brief Introduction to *The Urantia Book*

Rev. Dr. Meredith J. Sprunger

One of the greatest needs of contemporary society is to be inspired by a fresh and enlarged vision that will stimulate humankind to new spiritual growth. *The Urantia Book* is just such an epoch-making book. Like a mountain peak rising above the slumbering potentials of our contemporary scene, the book catches and reflects the light which signals the dawn of a new era. It seems destined to introduce unprecedented creative thought and action in the field of religion.

Such a claim surely will put a knowledgeable and responsible person on guard. Almost every generation produces a number of people who pose as bearers of a "new revelation." What is surprising about *The Urantia Book* is that it has almost nothing in common with radical or fanatical movements. Its viewpoint builds upon the religious heritage of the past and present; yet, it is fresh, expansive, and profound.

The high quality of the philosophical-religious insights of *The Urantia Book* is clear to anyone of discriminating mind who reads it. After a judicious and reflective reading of the book, one is impressed by the power of its own authenticity. It is a book, however, which cannot be adequately evaluated until one grasps its comprehensive universe cosmology—its total religious picture. And just as students of the life of Jesus recognize the superlative quality of his character even though they may reject his divinity, so humankind will eventually recognize the unparalleled quality of the insights of *The Urantia Book*—even though they do not accept is as a new revelation.

Revelatory authenticity, however, is a secondary consideration. The basic challenge posed by this stimulating book is pragmatic. Does it have something creative and constructive to contribute to our modern outlook? There is little question but that it can and will make a significant contribution to our religious thinking. Evaluated on the basis of spiritual insight, philosophic coherence, and reality-centeredness, it presents the finest worldview of religion available in our day. It will profoundly impress those who are interested in progressive philosophical and religious thinking which has the potential of molding world destiny.

A Holistic Philosophical Orientation

The philosophical-religious teaching of *The Urantia Book* includes an integrated and masterful concept of reality. The gap between monistic and pluralistic metaphysical concepts is bridged. Mechanistic and vitalistic interpretations of natural phenomena are integrated. Science and religion are seen as aspects of a larger unity. Concepts of deity ranging from that of a personal universal father to an impersonal absolute are so well unified that the holistic picture is harmonious.

An organized astronomical universe is projected that includes millions of inhabited planets in all stages of physical, intellectual, and spiritual evolution. The book contains what is probably the most realistic and inclusive material-mindal-spiritual cosmology in the entire field of philosophy and religion.

Moreover, *The Urantia Book* presents an eminently reasonable picture of the conditions and nature of immortality. Survival is seen as dependent on the spiritual status of the individual—the result of the free-choice motivation and decisions of the person toward truth, beauty, and goodness (God) as he or she sincerely understands these values. Nevertheless, evil, sin, and judgment are stern and sober realities in the universe.

In addition, the interrelationships of body, mind, soul, and spirit are treated with much insight and originality. The central challenge to modern humanity is to make a balanced effort to achieve God-consciousness, it teaches. Growth toward perfection is presented as the fundamental motivation of life. This growth is evolutionary, culminating, and virtually endless.

The Urantia Book also presents a superior understanding of planetary history, dynamics, and destiny. Evolution is seen as the key *modus operandi* of our planet. A summary of the development of religion and the growth of civilization is given with admirable conciseness and insight. The book's penetrating analysis of religion, culture, and the family is of exceptional quality. Its basic philosophy of the various forms of energy is that matter is ultimately subject to mind and that mind is eventually controlled by spirit.

The last section of *The Urantia Book* contains an extended version of the life and teachings of Jesus which in my opinion is unsurpassed in theistic philosophical reasonableness, spiritual insight, and personality appeal. This superb presentation of the life of Jesus brings life to the sketchy New Testament story and with it a new authenticity. It is basically acceptable to all religions, emphasizing the religion of Jesus which is unifying as opposed to the religion about Jesus which tends to be divisive.

A Resource Not an Imperative

Religious institutions usually find expanded knowledge and insight difficult to assimilate. Light can blind as well as guide. Truth that is presented prematurely brings frustration and rejection. *The Urantia Book*, therefore, may be disturbing to some people even though it is supportive and positive toward all people and all human efforts in the search for truth and spiritual understanding.

People are receptive to progressive spiritual values long before they are prepared to understand the origin and implications of these truths. Religious leaders, therefore, might best stimulate spiritual growth by translating the insights they discover in *The Urantia Book* into the idiom and reference frame of the people they serve. Even though *The Urantia Book* is among the most significant sources of spiritual guidance available to contemporary humankind, it is not an end in itself; nor is it a necessary means to spiritual enlightenment. Its potentials for individual and social growth, however, are so great it should be highly recommended to all who are interested in the creative possibilities of a spiritual renaissance in our society. Its message is balanced and profound. Its approach is open and benign. There are no threats or coercions to "believe." It seeks to work in and through the evolutionary process and within the social institutions of our world. During the years since its publication, this book, without advertisement or sales promotion, is being discovered by steadily increasing numbers of people. The overwhelming consensus among those who have discovered *The Urantia Book* is that it is destined for universal recognition on our planet.

The Urantia Book as a Compensatory Gift to Humankind

Byron Belitsos

This essay is excerpted from the author's most recent book,
Truths About Evil, Sin, and Iniquity—*perhaps the
first title from a mainstream academic publisher that
in part expounds* The Urantia Book.

Byron Belitsos, the general editor and publisher of this anthology, is a veteran book publisher and the award-winning author or editor of many books, including four related to the Urantia revelation: *The Center Within* (1998); *The Adventure of Being Human* (2012); *Your Evolving Soul* (2017); and an academic work entitled *Truths About Evil, Sin, and Iniquity* (Wipf & Stock, 2023). He holds a B.A. in history of ideas from the University of Chicago and an M.A. degree from Union Theological Seminary focused on theology and philosophy. A student of the *UB* for almost five decades, Byron has taught or spoken on its teachings in numerous venues nationwide.

The *Urantia Book*, a massive and enigmatic text, is known worldwide for its sophisticated Trinitarian theology and complex evolutionary cosmology—as well as for its unique depiction of evolutionary deity, its intricate discourses on religion, its integrative model of spirituality, and its exclusive revelations about planetary history and destiny.

The *UB*'s futuristic multiverse astronomy describes in unprecedented detail the diversity of intelligent life—both human and angelic—not only on our world, but also on higher worlds and on untold billions of inhabited material planets spread out across the evolving domains it calls the "grand universe."[3]

The vast grand universe is depicted as teeming with life and intricately organized. For example, the *UB* goes to great lengths to explain the workings and establish the legitimacy of what it calls "the universe government," providing unique detail that explains how it operates at its multiple levels.

The *UB* is best known, however, for its audacious retelling of the life and teachings of Jesus. This narrative adds considerable new detail to episodes recorded in the Gospels and offers a modernized "Jesusonian" spirituality, one that it purports to be the religion *of* Jesus rather than a religion *about* him. It sets aside a few outdated dogmas such as the atonement doctrine and the virgin birth while still affirming a substantively Chalcedonian theology.

According to *The Urantia Book*'s teaching, humans are potentially co-creative participants in our own personal growth as well as in the celestial governance of our planet. We are told that crucial but unseen ministries to each of us are carried out by diverse beings of light. These angels and celestials "reach down" for partnership with those faith-filled human collaborators who are reaching up for guidance and enlightenment. And yet, these invisible helpers are *not* infallible. That is, while being vastly more advanced than humans, they are created as less-than-perfect and non-eternal creatures (but technically future-eternal). At lower levels, these angelic ministers and administrators can go astray in ways that result in very rare instances of rebellion that drastically impact the welfare of the innocent humans who are their wards and co-workers. These higher beings are themselves free-will creatures who have been known to betray the local universe government, and indeed have done so in our local system and on our world, as described in detail in the Urantia text.

---

[3] The text depicts the mode of celestial governance of these worlds at different scales (including: inhabited planets, systems or constellations of planets,"local universes," and entire galaxies). Its coverage extends to *all* inhabited material galaxies (known as the *grand universe*), the trillions of galaxies still uninhabited, plus the "higher" worlds outside of time and space (altogether constituting the *master universe*).

According to its allegedly superhuman authors and editors, the Urantia text is an epochal disclosure of divine truth that has been provided to humankind as an *emergency measure*. The revelators (i.e., the multiple celestial authors of the *UB*) explain their gift in this way: "Times of great testing and threatened defeat are always times of great revelation" (195:9.3).

Starkly put, I believe we should open to new revelation at this time because our world needs and indeed has earned what I would call a rescue and salvage operation. I like to refer to such a divine outreach effort as the *compensatory nature* of divine revelation. The death-dealing adversity that results from the presence of radical evil—as evidenced in the genocides of recent history and the current existential threat of planetary ecocide—invites God's mercy as recompense. And such divine "reparation" is in accord with the mandates of God's love and justice.

In particular, when a planet is nearing the very extinction of its native life, the heart of the Creator is aroused and is moved to call forth urgent measures such as new revelation or even a new divine visitation. The sovereign God of love, the very source of planetary life, finds cause to intercede to console his children and conserve the vast riches of previous natural and human evolution, doing so while respecting the relative sovereignty of human free will.

Such a meeting of great opposites—that is, a compensatory revelatory response to adversity and horrendous evil—may remind us of the famed dialectic of G. W. F. Hegel, the nineteenth century German philosopher. According to Hegel, the "labor of the negative" in human history paradoxically yields positive outcomes: negation allows new and higher realities co-emerge along a spiral of progress toward greater goods. At each turn, a constructive and revelatory new "other" comes into view, even as what is no longer useful is discarded. Each "negation" shatters present arrangements and pushes toward a new dispensation, but it also conserves those hard-won truths or conditions of life worth retaining.

We might also call this the *dialectic of divine compensation*. Planetary trauma opens the way for "a negation of the negation," leading to new disclosures and a higher synthesis that may, for example, include a new worldview more suitable for our time, which I believe the Urantia revelation supplies. Yet it is important to bear in mind that such encounters with new negations (destabilizing "others" such as extraterrestrial life) are also virtually inexhaustible, such that any given step in the spiral will lead to still other unknowns.

It is worth noting that this dialectical pattern of divine compensation is also present in biblical narratives:

- Dramatic divine intervention delivered the Jews from bondage at the moment when the scourge of slavery had become intolerable. "And God spoke all these words: '*I am* the Lord your *God, who brought you out of Egypt,* out of the land of slavery'" (Ex 20:2-3).

- A millennium later, when the messianic expectation of the Hebrews was peaking in the face of the unbearable pain of Roman occupation, Jesus appeared to offer deliverance—but of a sort few had anticipated.

- Jesus himself alludes to the dialectic of divine recompense in his Olivet Discourse that occurs just before the Passion, where he explains to the Apostles the compensatory action of his Father at a future time of greatest tribulation: "For then there will be great distress, unequaled from the beginning of the world until now—and never to be equaled again. . . . Then will appear the sign of the Son of Man in heaven. And then all the peoples of the earth will . . . see the Son of Man coming on the clouds of heaven, with power and great glory" (Matt 24:21-30).

And one can think of numerous other examples of how an unexpected "presencing" of the holy—such as the Marian apparition at Fatima in the midst of the horrors of World War I—becomes an instrument of compensation for suffering or even may act as the source of unexpected healing.

In this light, it is a remarkable fact that the original manuscript of the Urantia Revelation was completed in 1945, just as Western civilization had reached its nadir. In this same moment, the horrors of WWII were coming to light as a shocked world looked on.[4]

The "neo-supernaturalism" of the Urantia Revelation itself can be seen as merciful recompense for two world wars that culminated in the atrocities of WWII, the Holocaust, and the nuclear bomb attacks on Japan. Here again was a form of divine response few had anticipated, provided at a time of great testing.[5]

I regard *The Urantia Book* to be a compensatory gift to humankind that broadly addresses the issues entailed in the horrendous evils of the last century, among its many other important functions. It helps us address our current trajectory into a very uncertain future even while it offers assurances of better times ahead in the far future.

---

[4] The final preparations of the Urantia text are said to have been made that year. The book was not published, however, until a decade later. Researchers believe that the latest human source whose ideas were incorporated into the manuscript (at 134:3) is Emery Reves, author of the bestselling 1945 book, *The Anatomy of Peace*. *(For an explanation of the methodology of the incorporation of the ideas of human authors, see* the upcoming discussion on "human sources.") Reves's advocacy for a world federal government that would abolish war and establish a global constitution, world courts, and a world parliament was a prophetic call for justice that was largely ignored and at times actively opposed in the post-war world. And yet the *UB* not only extols this concept but makes clear that, if he were alive today, Jesus would support such an approach to global governance.

[5] We might compare this result to the influential neo-Orthodoxy movement led by German theologian Karl Barth in the aftermath of the previous war. Barth was horrified by the capitulation of the mainstream German church to those nationalist forces that plunged the country into WWI. A generation later, a large portion of the church went on to support the Nazi movement. Barth's theological movement has thrived ever since as a correction to the moral lapses of liberal German theology that seemed to have opened the doors of the German apocalypse.

The Great Adventure: Man in Partnership with God

William Sadler, Jr

In this transcribed speech presented to the Urantia Society of Oklahoma City in 1958, William Sadler, Jr., offers reflections on what The Urantia Book *has meant to him after a lifetime of study.*

William Sadler, Jr. (December 15, 1907 – November 22, 1963) was the only child of the original founders of the Urantia movement, Dr. William S. Sadler and Dr. Lena Sadler. While his parents were both physicians, William worked in various industry positions and later founded Sadler & Associates, a business management consultancy based in downtown Chicago. The junior Sadler is best known as a prominent member of the two groups that originated the revelation: the Forum and the Contact Commissioners (both described in chapter 5). Bill

William Sadler, Jr

Sadler, Jr., better known as "Bill," was a gifted student of *The Urantia Book* with a special talent for distilling its most complex teachings into conversational language, which this speech puts on display. Bill was considered a natural-born teacher, and along with his father instructed the first groups organized for systematic study. He was one of the original trustees of the Urantia Foundation and the first President of the Urantia Brotherhood, and also authored *A Study of the Master Universe* and *Appendices to A Study of the Master Universe*, masterworks that provide advanced and substantive analyses of the *UB*'s cosmological and theological teachings.

This being something of an open meeting of the Urantia Society, I pondered at length what I could talk to you about that would be most interesting and most useful to all of you. If we were to talk about the facts of *The Urantia Book*, I think I could cover that in about six months of intensive discussion. Or, we can discuss the meanings that can be derived from these facts, and I suppose that could be covered in about two years. But instead I thought I would share my feelings for this book—not the facts, not the meanings—but what value this book has provided in my life as a human being here on earth. So I picked as a title for this discussion, "The Great Adventure—Man in Partnership with God. "

This book appeals to me because it presents the story of evolution in contrast to fiat creation. God can, and does, work apart from time, but when he works apart from time, no creature can participate in that development. However, when God works in time, he slows down the creative process to something we call evolutionary growth, and this enables a creature—even a human being—to sense what is happening, and if he so elects, to go in partnership with God, to become a partner in this growth process.

I like the idea of sharing in the creative adventure with Deity, and when I speak of partnership with God, I mean no disrespect; I know I am the junior partner and God is the senior partner, but there is a difference when you are a partner. Even if you are a junior partner, you have something to say about policy. I don't change God's mind, but it is my decision as to whether or not he can change my mind.

How does God equip his junior partners—human beings? Well, quite obviously, we have bodies and minds, but these don't come from God. What equipment does God give us that indicates he is willing to enter into any kind of a limited partnership with us? Well, he gives us two priceless pieces of equipment.

First of all, he gives us an absolute sense of direction; he incarcerates a part of his love inside of us. He lives in us, even as the Bible says, as "the true light which lighteth every man that cometh into the world. " This part of God that lives in us is God's love made real to each one of us, and this part of God that lives in us knows the way to God. It points just as unerringly God-ward as a compass needle points northward. It came from God, so it knows the way back to God. It is our unerring pilot.

And God gives us a second priceless endowment—he endows us with relative free will, freedom of choice. The pilot [God's Indwelling Spirit] is not the captain. We are captain because of our free will. The pilot can steer only as we choose.

If I think of all the priceless gifts that God could make to me, none would transcend this endowment of freedom of choice. Otherwise, I would be a machine. With freedom of choice, I am a person. I can be a son of God. What else does freedom of choice mean? It means that I just don't have to respond slavishly to what happens to me. I have something to say about what I become. Even physically, I have something to say. I can't avoid wrinkles, but I can choose which kind will etch themselves into my face. I can frown or I can smile.

In the sense that I have relative freedom of will, I am made in the image of God. I have been liberated from marching in lock-step to antecedent causation. This book teaches me that the more outside of myself I go toward the material level, the less choosing I can do. For example, I can't choose to be older or younger. But the more I move inward away from the material level, inward and spiritward, the greater is my liberation of choice. This continues until I reach the supreme choice, pro or con concerning God, and here my choice knows no restriction. Regarding my decision as to whether I choose to be His son, to do His will—I am absolutely on my own. Here my choice is absolute. God has given us this perfectly splendid equipment—freedom of choice and an absolute sense of direction. We can't miss if we let the pilot do a good steering job.

At the same time, God has confronted us with a great challenge. All religions teach this challenge, and it is expressed in various forms. The challenge presented by medieval Christianity was not so much the hope of heaven as it was the fear of the devil in hell. I think that is still true today; many people operate on a negative basis. I recall a friend of mine who returned a piece of stolen merchandise—it was a wrist watch—and he returned it because he had a dream, and in this dream he saw himself sitting on a red-hot rock in the eternal tropics, looking at a wrist watch that was calibrated in cycles of eternity.

This book teaches me I have a challenge, but it is not the challenge of fear—it is the challenge of a situation. This book tells me that I am confronted with this kind of a challenge, and I quote the book—"In the evolutionary universes, energy-matter is dominant, save in personality, where spirit, through the mediation of mind is striving for the mastery." That is a rather long sentence; let's break it down. Energy-matter is here first. Just consider our planet. It passed through its astro-physical evolution before life ever appeared, and it has been around here for several billion years. Life has been here for only a fraction of that time.

Human life has been around here for only about a million years, less than a tenth of one percent of physical planetary history, and when man did appear on earth, he was confronted with a rather hostile material environment. He had to adjust to it, strive to dominate it, in order to survive.

Mind can whip matter because mind can be ingenious, it can manipulate matter. But that is not the challenge. The challenge is: can *spirit* dominate matter, using mind as its tool? And this challenge holds true only in personality, in the special way this book defines it. How come? Only in personality, which possesses this priceless endowment of free will, can mind choose to attack matter on the outside, while at the same time subordinating itself to spirit direction on the inside.

This book gives me a mature philosophy of religion, it gives me a theology that is spiritually satisfying and at the same time intellectually stimulating. This book enables me to avoid the two great errors that cut right across human thinking all over this world. Error No. 1—"You strive with spirit alone—spirit without mind." If you really believe this, you will substitute prayer for work. This is the error fundamental both in Hinduism and the southern school of Buddhism. This is also an error our Christian Science friends enjoy.

When you attack the problems of living with spirit alone, you are forced to deny the reality of matter, and you wind up with a theology full of illusion. The Hindu has a name for the illusion of matter—he calls it "Maya"—which means it's not really there. He trusts everything is spirit and simply says "the world is not here." Theravada Buddhism does the same thing. I love the story they tell about three Buddhist monks in various stages of enlightenment. Each monk is sitting by the side of the road with his begging bowl in front of him, and, of course, what the monks in their saffron robes beg for is food, not money. The first monk looks down in his begging bowl and he sees three hairs—a very, very repugnant sight—"I don't like the idea of hair in my eating equipment." They bother him. These three hairs symbolize the illusory reality of the material world. The second monk is farther along in the process of enlightenment—he sees the hairs, but they don't bother him because he knows they aren't real. The third monk? He doesn't see the hairs.

Now, there is an alternative to this, and all too many people, especially occidental people, fall victim to this second alternative; this is to attack the physical problems of this world with mind alone, without spirit. This is at the root of secularism. Consider the medieval Christian viewpoint. Let's take the city of Florence—pre-renaissance Florence. The plague hits the city, and the devout Christian Florentine bows his head as he buries his loved ones and says: "The Lord giveth, the Lord taketh away, blessed be the name of the Lord."

Comes the Renaissance and men begin to rebel against this passive acceptance of material happenstance, and in their rebellion they swing all the way in the other direction. They become secularists—*man* is now the measure of all things. I don't look down my nose at the fruits of secularism—this has resulted in modern science, representative government, relatively universal education, the highest standard of living we have ever had—but something is also wrong. With all of our unprecedented material progress, have men ever been so scared as they are today?

When mind attacks the problem without spirit, it progresses, but its progress is thwarted and jeopardized by selfishness, by fear, by lack of ethics and morality and love. We can't successfully run a free society without God anymore than you could run the solar system without gravity.

I'm sorry for my Hindu and Buddhist friends who say "the world is an illusion—I'll do it all with prayer and meditation." I tremble for the future of our secularistic society which is trying to work out all these problems with *mind alone*. What a harvest of fear we are reaping. You know, that in my lifetime, in major wars, we have scientifically killed off more human beings than have been killed in all the recorded history of war. There is something wrong with secularism, isn't there? But the alternative is not merely a "spiritistic" society. This book tells me that when you conjoin mind and spirit, you can have peace on earth, survival in death, and in your afterlife in the cosmos you can have the great adventure.

This is the most sane philosophy I have ever encountered. It presents no easy path to peace on earth or salvation in the future—it offers lots of hard work.

Matter presents a challenge to each of us. The task of mind is to develop the techniques for solving this challenge of the reality of physical mass energy. What are we doing on this planet to civilize it? What is a pipeline, but an artery? What is a telegraph wire, but a nerve? We are doing to this planet what a contractor does to a sub-division when he takes rolling hills and dales and makes them habitable through bringing in utilities, conveniences, and so on. Matter challenges us—mind develops the technique—and spirit provides the motivation. Without spirit direction, this problem-solving mind eventually winds up in a cul-de-sac of hate, fear, jealousy, and perhaps death.

I was born in Chicago—I love my city. It has the magnificence of civilization aborning all about it. Carl Sandburg well called it "hog-butcher to the world." It's a beautiful city, too. I work amidst the facade of skyscrapers along the lakefront. It has taken Americans nearly 150 years to build this city, but it can be blown to hell in 150 minutes with the techniques we have developed today. I ponder that, and I know fear. Without spiritual motivation, mind can be a juggernaut—a Frankenstein's monster—because it knows power, and it can know power without restraint.

It is personality—it's this equipment God has given us—that can choose to subordinate this questing, adventurous, and problem-solving mind to the direction of spirit. We can meet this mortal challenge without committing human suicide.

I don't think there is anything magical or mystical about Western civilization. I have studied history. Rome went down, Babylon went down, Assyria went down. China has gone down half a dozen times. Egypt broke up, and Greece came and went. I don't think we have any guarantee of the future. In the struggle in which we are engaged right now, I don't think material techniques are enough. The biggest thing that is missing in American ideology is God. We are never going to beat our competitors by a way of life that involves more mustard and piccalilli on our hot dogs and more chrome plating on our automobiles.

These Urantia Papers tell me that one of the great things that is taking place out here in these evolutionary universes is the unification of power and personality. This is what we have been discussing. As mind dominates matter—this is power. And, that mind which dominates matter is the mind of a choosing personality. But if this powerful person is to persist, he must be spirit-motivated. Force alone never survives. No matter how much force you mobilize, eventually your power begets fear and there arises a coalition stronger than you are which drags you down in defeat.

What is the effect of spirit on power—meaning for example a powerful person? If a powerful person is spirit motivated—and he can choose to be so—then he is an ethical person, he is a moral person; he uses power with restraint. The power he possesses causes him to be an object of admiration, not fear. He is a love-motivated individual. And this book defines love very wonderfully—"Love is the desire to do good to others." Such an individual lives up to one of the really great quotes from this book—"To have power and refuse to use it purely for selfish aggrandizement, this is the mark of a high civilization."

This challenge is the challenge that comes from a loving God, but not a soft God. God's love is not a soft love—it is a stimulating love. It is like the love of a wise parent who would never do a child's homework for him until the child had exhausted his own efforts. This challenge is well stated by the book when it says: "The weak make resolutions, but strong men act. Life is but a day's work, do it well. The act is ours—the consequences, God's."

Jesus lived such a life. Jesus was an intensely practical man. Among other things, he said "Render unto Caesar the things which are Caesar's." We tend to forget that half of the quote, don't we? He said "Cast not your pearls before swine." These are not the statements you might get from a starry-eyed impractical dreamer. The Christ that we paint anemic pictures of might just possibly have appealed to the Ladies Aid

Society of Capernaum, but he could have never carried those hard-boiled fishermen with him. He told his followers to be as "wise as serpents" as well as "harmless as doves." When they didn't have any money in the treasury, did he say, "Shall we pray?" He said "No, we will go fishing and we will sell the fish and finance ourselves, and then we will go preach."

He was a good carpenter in Nazareth and he worked for money, he didn't pray for it. Incidentally, he was such a good carpenter that even when there was a depression, he had plenty of work to do. He didn't just "sprangle" through Galilee and Judea with twelve fellows—he organized them. They had jobs to do. It was a simple but effective organization. He didn't just take these twelve men up on the mountain, place hands on them, imbue them with power from on high and say "Go spread the message." No! He gave these twelve men between four and five years of the most intelligently practical sales training I know anything about.

When he finished with them, he tested them, and he commissioned nine of them to spread the good news. One was dead, and two he sent back to the fishing nets. He recognized human differences; he knew that prayer couldn't change a man's IQ. He gave Peter one set of instructions. He gave the Alpheus twins, who weren't very bright but very lovable, another set of instructions. To Peter, he said, "Be a good shepherd, feed my sheep." To these slow-thinking but wonderful Alpheus twins, he said: "Boys, go back to your fish nets, and remember, to a God-knowing kingdom believer, there is no such thing as secular work. All work is sacred." I see this union of mind and spirit best exemplified in the inspiring but intensely practical life of Joshua ben Joseph, whom we know as Jesus of Nazareth.

When mind attacks matter, you get skill. I feel sorry for people who have no real skill, who are not really professional in doing something. You know, I would rather be awfully good at drilling dry holes than to drill sloppy holes. That language, I think, is good semantics in Oklahoma, isn't it? When you turn the mind loose to attack the problems of matter, you get skill. Now, when you subordinate mind to spirit, you get love. And when you combine love and skill—when you combine problem-solving ability with the desire to do good to others—you get something pretty wonderful—you get wisdom. From a temporal standpoint, considering everything below the level of spirit, I think wisdom is the pearl of great price. If we have this kind of wisdom, we can attack the stimulating adventure of this life with courage, with tenderness, with worship, with humor. That is an unbeatable combination.

And so, as I distill the teachings of this book—not the facts, not the meanings, but the value—I see wisdom in this life, sonship with God in the next life, and forevermore spiritual growth in the business of knowing God, finding out more and more about him. This book well teaches me that God is the first truth and the last fact. He is the first divine reality that I can feel, but he is the last divine reality that I will ever understand because he is infinite. And I have the feeling that if we choose to use the mind's courage and the spirit's love wisely together in meeting the challenge of matter, we can enter upon a never-ending partnership with God. And this partnership is one of adventurous service in the execution of God's will in the ever-growing universes, throughout all the endless cycles of eternity.

PART II

ORIGIN STUDIES

Prologue II: Excerpts on the Origin of the Papers

66 Your world, Urantia, is one of many similar inhabited planets which comprise the local universe of *Nebadon*. This universe, together with similar creations, makes up the superuniverse of *Orvonton*, from whose capital, Uversa, our commission hails. Orvonton is one of the seven evolutionary superuniverses of time and space which circle the never-beginning, never-ending creation of divine perfection—the central universe of *Havona*. At the heart of this eternal and central universe is the stationary Isle of Paradise, the geographic center of infinity and the dwelling place of the eternal God. 99   (0:0.5)

66 Successive planetary revelations of divine truth invariably embrace the highest existing concepts of spiritual values as a part of the new and enhanced co-ordination of planetary knowledge. Accordingly, in making these presentations about God and his universe associates, we have selected as the basis of these papers more than one thousand human concepts representing the highest and most advanced planetary knowledge of spiritual values and universe meanings. Wherein these human concepts, assembled from the God-knowing mortals of the past and the present, are inadequate to portray the truth as we are directed to reveal it, we will unhesitatingly supplement them, for this purpose drawing upon our own superior knowledge of the reality and divinity of the Paradise Deities and their transcendent residential universe. 99   (0:12.10)

66 Acknowledgment: In carrying out my commission to restate the teachings and retell the doings of Jesus of Nazareth, I have drawn freely upon all sources of record and planetary information. My ruling motive has been to prepare a record which will not only be enlightening to the generation of men now living, but which may also be helpful to all future generations. From the vast store of information made available to me, I have chosen that which is best suited to the accomplishment of this purpose. As far as possible I have derived my information from purely human sources. Only when such sources failed, have I resorted to those records which are superhuman. When ideas and concepts of Jesus' life and teachings have been acceptably expressed by a human mind, I invariably gave preference to such apparently human thought patterns. Although I have sought to adjust the verbal expression the better to conform to our concept of the real meaning and the true import of the Master's life and teachings, as far as possible, I have adhered to the actual human concept and thought pattern in all my narratives. I well know that those concepts which have had origin in the human mind will prove more acceptable and helpful to all other human minds. When unable to find the necessary concepts in the human records or in human expressions, I have next resorted to the memory resources of my own order of earth creatures, the midwayers. And when that secondary source of information proved inadequate, I have unhesitatingly resorted to the superplanetary sources of information. The memoranda which I have collected, and from which I have prepared this narrative of the life and teachings of Jesus—aside from the memory of the record of the Apostle Andrew—embrace thought gems and superior concepts of Jesus' teachings assembled from more than two thousand human beings who have lived on earth from the days of Jesus down to the time of the inditing of these revelations, more correctly restatements. The revelatory permission has been utilized only when the human record and human concepts failed to supply an adequate thought pattern. My revelatory commission forbade me to resort to extrahuman sources of either information or expression until such a time as I could testify that I had failed in my efforts to find the required conceptual expression in purely human sources. 99 (121:8.10)

5

A History of the Urantia Movement

The Contact Commission
June 30, 1960

The following account, slightly abridged and lightly copyedited, is the first of several histories of the early movement, and represents the exclusive point of view of the so-called Contact Commissioners, a group based in Chicago who were the actual witnesses of these events.

The Contact Commission is the original group of six men and women who were the direct contactees for the invisible celestial revelators of the Urantia Papers, beginning as far back as 1911. They have come to be known as the "Contact Commissioners." They were charged by

The Contact Commission (from left to right): Emma "Christy" Christensen, Lena Sadler, William S. Sadler, Bill Sadler, Anna and Wilfred Kellogg

the superhuman directors of the revelatory process to be present at preliminary sessions convened over many years in which an unconscious man, the so-called "contact personality," transmitted communications from the revelators. The subsequent task of the Commissioners was to become the custodians of the original Papers that later became *The Urantia Book*. To this day the identity of the contact personality, also known as "the sleeping subject," has remained a secret known only to the Contact Commissioners, the last of whom passed in 1982.

Several members of our group who participated in the preliminary "contacts" had considerable experience in the investigation of psychic phenomena. This group early arrived at the conclusion that the phenomena connected with the personality who was later associated with the Urantia Papers was in no way similar to any other well-known type of psychic performance—such as hypnosis, automatic writing, clairvoyance, trances, spirit mediumship, telepathy, or double personality. It should be made clear that the antecedents of the Urantia Papers were in no way associated with so-called spiritualism—with its seances and supposed communication with spirits of departed human beings.

Contact Activities Preceding the Urantia Papers

It would seem that, during the early years [*circe* 1911 to 1932], our unseen friends, also known as the "Revelatory Commission," were engaged in a thoroughgoing testing of the contact personality. They were rehearsing the technique of communication as well as selecting the Contact Commissioners—and, in fact, in a general way—setting the stage for the subsequent initiation of the presentation of the Urantia Papers. During these early years we were introduced to many new and, to us, somewhat strange concepts of the universe of universes and as concerned man and his life on earth. Among these numerous new ideas of cosmology and philosophy, the following may be mentioned:

1. A new concept of a far-flung cosmos

2. Millions of other inhabited planets

3. Introduction to scores of varied echelons of celestial personalities

4. Confirmation of the evolutionary origin of humankind—even of an evolutionary cosmos.

5. Intimation of multiple Creator Deities.

6. A tentative testing of our theologic concepts. The patient determination of how far we might possibly go in the direction of modifying our theologic beliefs and philosophical opinions.

7. Without realizing it, over a period of twenty years, our fundamental religious views and attitudes had been considerably changed.

8. We were familiarized with such terms as "The First Source and Center," "Havona," "superuniverses," and the "Supreme Being"—but we had but meager ideas as to the real meaning of these names.

9. We also heard such words as "Master Spirits," "outer space," and "Power Directors." But, again, we understood little as to their meaning. We also learned about numerous orders of angels.

10. We heard about "Thought Adjusters," but our concept of the meaning of the term was vague and indefinite.

11. We acquired a fuzzy concept of the morontia level of existence—but we never heard the word "morontia" used until the Papers started.

12. The midwayers were very real to us—we frequently talked with them during our varied "contacts." We quite fully understood that the secondary midwayers supervised the contacts.

13. We heard some things about the Lucifer rebellion, but got little information about Adam and Eve.

14. We gained the impression that there were special reasons for Jesus' bestowal on Urantia, but we had little or no idea as to the nature of these unrevealed reasons.

15. We listened to occasional references to Jesus' life and teachings—but they were very cautious about the introduction of any new concepts regarding Michael's Urantia bestowal. Of all the surprises connected to the Urantia Revelation, the Jesus Papers were the biggest.

Our superhuman friends thus spent upward of two decades in extending our cosmic horizons, enlarging our theologic concepts, and expanding our over-all philosophy.

We never realized how much our religious thinking had been expanded until the Papers began to arrive. As the Revelation progressed we came more fully to appreciate how we had been prepared for the vast alteration of our religious beliefs by these preliminary contacts extending over a period of twenty years of pre-education.

Our apprenticeship training for subsequent service in association with the presentation of the Urantia Papers was facilitated by the fact that, except for contacts with the midwayers, no two contacts were alike. Seldom did we meet the visiting personalities more than once. Every contact was entirely different from any and all that had gone before. And all of this experience was an extensive and liberal preparatory educational training in the expansion of our cosmology, theology, and philosophy—not to mention our introduction to new ideas and concepts concerning a vast array of more mundane objects.

The limited discussion of Jesus' life and teachings during these pre-revelatory contacts might be explained by the fact that the midwayers were a bit dubious as to how much authority they had in such matters—as shown later on when a whole year was consumed in the clarification of their right to retell the story of the Michael bestowal.

Those of us who early attended upon these nocturnal vigils never suspected that we were in contact with anything supernatural. During these early years, all of our observations and investigations utterly failed to reveal the revelators' technique of reducing messages to writing.

How the Urantia Papers Started

After about twenty years of contact experience, an alleged student visitor, speaking through this sleeping subject during one of these nocturnal vigils, in answer to one of our questions, said: "If you only knew what you are in contact with you would not ask such trivial questions. You would rather ask such questions as might elicit answers of supreme value to the human race."

This was something of a shock, as well as a mild rebuke, and caused all of us to look upon this unique experience in a new and different way. Later on that night, one of our number said: "Now they have asked for it—let us give them questions that no human being can answer." Now it is best to let matters rest here while we shift this narrative to a new and different setting.

How the Forum Started

Dr. William S. Sadler, a member of this early group of observers and investigators, tells the following story regarding the origin of that group of interested individuals that later on became known as the "Forum." He says: "On my way to the University of Kansas to deliver some lectures on Gestalt psychology, I wrote a letter to my son saying that I thought doctors should try to maintain some contact with their old patients. I suggested that he talk with his mother about the feasibility of inviting some of our old friends to meet with us on Sunday afternoons for an hour or two of informal discussion and social exchange. When I returned to Chicago one Sunday morning I found that my wife had invited a group of our old patients to meet at our house that afternoon at three o'clock. It was the plan to conduct these Sunday afternoon gatherings somewhat as follows: First have a talk on some health topic—such as the treatment of common colds, the cause and cure of worry, and then, after a cup of tea, engage in informal discussions—asking and answering questions."

As time passed, this group became a cosmopolitan gathering consisting of professional men and women—doctors, lawyers, dentists, ministers, teachers—together with individuals from all walks of life. These included farmers, housewives, secretaries, office workers, and common laborers.

Introduction of the Forum to the "Contacts"

Presently, Dr. Sadler was asked to give a series of talks on "Mental Hygiene," or "Psychic Phenomena." At the beginning of his first talk, he said: "With only or two exceptions, all of the psychic phenomena which I have investigated have turned out to be either conscious or unconscious frauds. Some were deliberate frauds—others were those peculiar cases in which the performer was a victim of the deceptions of his own subconscious mind."

Dr. Sadler goes on to narrate the events that followed: "I had no more than said this when one of the group spoke up, saying, 'Doctor, if you have contacted something which you have been unable to solve—it would be interesting—tell us more about it.' I asked Dr. Lena to get some notes she had taken at a recent 'contact' and read them to the group. It should be understood that up to this time there was no secrecy connected with this case. *The Urantia Papers* had not begun to appear. It was at about this time that this group meeting at our house on Sunday afternoons began to be called the 'Forum.' The group manifested such a great interest in this case that I never did get around to giving any of the health talks such as had been planned.

"It was while these informal discussions were going on from week to week that the challenge came to us suggesting that if we would ask more serious questions we might get information of value to all mankind."

The Forum Begins to Ask Questions

We told the Forum all about this and invited them to join us in the preparation of questions. We decided to start out with questions pertaining to the origin of the cosmos, Deity, creation, and such other subjects as were far beyond the present-day knowledge of all humankind.

The following Sunday several hundred questions were brought in. We sorted out these questions, discarding duplicates, and in a general way, classifying them. Shortly thereafter, the first Urantia Paper appeared in answer to these questions. From first to last, when the Papers appeared, the questions [physically] disappeared. This was the procedure followed throughout the many years of the reception of the *Urantia Papers*. No questions—no papers.

The Forum Becomes a Closed Group

About this time, the Forum, as it were, was taken away from us. We were instructed to form a "closed group"—requiring each member to sign a pledge of secrecy and to discuss the Papers and all matters pertaining thereto with only those persons who were members of the Forum. Membership tickets were issued and the Charter membership numbered thirty. The date of this organization was September, 1925. Seventeen of these Charter Members are still living.

The individuals charged with the responsibility of gathering up the questions and comparing the typewritten text with the original handwritten manuscript, came to be known as the "Contact Commissioners." From that date forward only these Contact Commissioners attended "contacts" and received written communications through the contact personality.

From time to time new members were received into the Forum, after being interviewed by the officers and after signing the same pledge that was signed by the original Charter Members. This pledge read: "We acknowledge our pledge of secrecy, renewing our promise not to discuss the Urantia Revelations or their subject matter with any one save active Forum members, and to take no notes of such matter as is read or discussed at the public sessions, or make copies or notes of what we personally read."

The last meeting of the Forum as a genetic assembly was held on May 31st, 1942. During the 17 years of official existence the Forum attained a total membership of 486. During the period of the reception of the Urantia Papers, upward of 300 different persons participated in asking these genetic questions. With but few exceptions, all of the Urantia Papers were given in response to such questions.

How We Got the Urantia Papers

Just about all that is known or could be told about the origin of the Urantia Papers is to be found, here and there, in *The Urantia Book*. A list of such references is to be found on the back of the dust jacket of the Book.

Let us take a brief look at these citations, which are paraphrased in the list below:

1. Page 1, par. 2. This passage refers to the difficulty of presenting expanded spiritual concepts when restricted to circumscribed human language, such as English.

2. Page 1, par. 4. An Orvonton Commission participated in the revelation and prepared this Foreword.

3. Page 17, par. 1. In presenting this revelation of augmented spiritual values and universe meanings, more than one thousand human concepts were drawn from the minds of human beings of the present and the past.

4. Page 16, par. 8 and page 1343, par. 1. In all revelation of truth, preference is given to the highest existing human concepts of

ideality and reality. Only in the absence of the human concept is superhuman knowledge revealed.

5. Page 1109, par. 4. Revelators are seldom at liberty to anticipate scientific discoveries. Truth is timeless, but the teachings respecting the physical sciences and certain phases of cosmology will become partially obsolescent as a result of the new discoveries of advancing scientific investigations. The cosmology of the Urantia Revelation is not inspired. Human wisdom must evolve.

6. Page 215, par. 2-9 Human pedagogy proceeds from the simple to the complex. The Urantia Revelation begins with the more complex and goes on to the consideration of the more simple. Instead of beginning with man reaching up for God, the Urantia Papers begin with God—reaching down and finding man.

7. Page 865. par. 6, 7 The narrative of the midwayers function in initiating and carrying forward to completion the Urantia Revelation.

8. Page 865, par. 2, & Page 1208, par. 7. Midway creatures are always employed in the phenomenon of communication with material beings through the technique of "Contact Personalities." The "subject" through whom the Urantia Papers were bestowed had a highly experienced Thought Adjuster. The "subject's" relative indifference and unconcern regarding the work of his indwelling Adjuster was in every way favorable to the execution and completion of this revelatory project.

9. Page 1256, par. 1. The contact personality was a member of the Urantia Reserve Corps of Destiny. This was just one of several conditions favoring the impartation of the Urantia Revelation.

10. Page 1008, par. 3. The Urantia Revelation is unique in that it is presented by multiple authors. The Urantia Revelation, like its predecessors, is not inspired.

11. Page 32, par.2. A Divine Counselor "portrays the reality and nature of the Father with unchallengeable authority."

12. Page 17, par. 2. The Revelators depend upon the indwelling Adjusters and the Spirit of Truth to help us in the appropriation of the truth in the Urantia Revelation.

13. Page 1007, par. 1. Revelation keeps in touch with evolution. Revelation is adapted to the age of its bestowal. New revelation maintains contact with preceding revelations.

Reason for Silence Respecting Details of the Origin of *The Urantia Book*

Among the several reasons given us at the time we were requested not to discuss the details of our personal experiences associated with the origin of *The Urantia Book*, the two major reasons were the following:

1. *Unknown features.* There is much connected with the appearance of the Urantia Papers which no human being fully understands. None of us really knows just how this phenomenon was executed. There are numerous missing links in our understanding of how this revelation came to appear in written English. If any one of us should tell any one all he really knows about the technique and methods employed throughout the years of our getting this Revelation, such a narration would satisfy no one—there are too many missing links.

2. *Identity of the contact personality.* The main reason for not revealing the identity of the contact person is that the revelators do not want any human being—any human name—ever to be associated with *The Urantia Book*. They want this revelation to stand on its own declarations and teachings. They are determined that future generations shall have the book wholly free from all mortal connections—they do not want a Saint Peter, Saint Paul, Luther, Calvin, or Wesley. The book does not even bear the imprint of the printer who brought the book into being. Remember: You could appreciate a good poem—even if you did not know the author. Likewise, you could enjoy a symphony even if you were ignorant of the composer.

The First Urantia Papers

The first group of Papers numbered 57. We then received a communication suggesting that since we could now ask many and much more intelligent questions, the supervising agencies and personalities responsible for transmitting the 57 Papers would engage to enlarge the revelation and to expand the Papers in accordance with our new questions.

This was the plan: We would read a Paper on a Sunday afternoon and the following Sunday the new questions would be presented. Again, these would be sorted, classified, etc. This program covered several years and ultimately resulted in the presentation of the 196 Papers as now found in *The Urantia Book*.

Receiving the Completed Papers

In a way, there was a third presentation. After receiving these 196 Papers, we were told that the Revelatory Commission would be pleased to have us go over the Papers once more and ask questions concerning the "clarification of concepts" and the "removal of ambiguities." This program again covered several years. During this period very little new information was imparted. Only minor changes were made in any of the Papers. Some matter was added—some removed—but there was little revision or amplification of the text.

What has just been stated refers more particularly to Parts I, II, and III of *The Urantia Book*. Part IV—The Jesus Papers—had a little different origin. They were produced by a midwayer commission and were completed one year later than the other Papers. The first three parts were completed and certified to us in A.D. 1934. The Jesus Papers were not so delivered to us until 1935.

The Delay in Receiving the Jesus Papers

The delay of one year in the reception of the Jesus Papers—Part IV of *The Urantia Book*—may be explained as follows: The midwayers were a bit apprehensive about becoming involved in the suit pending in the universe courts—*Gabriel vs. Lucifer*—and they hesitated to complete their project until they were assured that they had full authority to retell the story of Jesus' life on earth.

After some months waiting there came the mandate from Uversa directing the United Midwayers of Urantia to proceed with their project of revealing the story of the life and teaching of Michael when incarnated on Urantia, and not only assuring them that they were not in "contempt" of the Uversa courts, but instead granting them a mandate to do this service and admonishing any and all persons connected therewith to refrain from interfering with, or in any way hindering, the execution of such an undertaking. And this is the explanation of why the Jesus Papers appear one year after the other Papers had been completed.

Functioning of the Contact Commissioners

During these early years the Contact Commissioners received many communications and directives in writing. Almost all of these messages had annotation at the bottom of the last page which read: "To be destroyed by fire not later than the appearance of the Urantia Papers in print." It was the design of our unseen friends to prevent the appearance of an "Urantia Apocrypha" subsequent to the publication of *The Urantia Book*. All of this was encouraging to us in that it assured us that the Urantia Papers would some time be published. It sustained our hopes through the long waiting years of delay.

The fact that no provision was ever made for replacing members of the Contact Commission who might be lost through disability or death, also led us to entertain the belief that the Book would be published during the lifetime of some of us.

The Commissioners were the custodians of the Urantia manuscript, keeping the carbon copy of the typewritten transcript in a fireproof vault. They were also charged with full responsibility for supervising all the details connected with the publication of the Book, securing the international copyrights, etc.

We were enjoined to refrain from discussing the identity of the contact personality and, after the publication of the Book, to make any statement at any time as to whether the "subject" was still living or was deceased.

The Seventy

In 1939, some of us thought the time had come when we should form a class to engage in the more serious and systematic study of the Urantia Papers. This project was presented to the Forum and when those who wished to join such a group were counted, it was found that just 70 persons desired to enter upon this study. So for several years this class was referred to as "The Seventy." Two or three years preceding the formation of The Seventy an informal group had been meeting on Wednesday evenings.

The Seventy carried on systematic study of the Urantia Papers from April 3, 1939 to the summer of 1956, and was the forerunner of the later "School of the Urantia Brotherhood." During these years the Seventy enrolled 107 students.

The Seventy carried on its work of study, thesis writing, and practice of teaching for 17 years. During this period eight written communications were given to the Seventy by the Seraphim of Progress attached to the superhuman Planetary Government of Urantia.

The Publication Mandate

At long last, permission to publish the Urantia Papers was granted. The Introduction to this mandate reads:

"We regard *The Urantia Book* as a feature of the progressive evolution of human society. It is not germane to the spectacular episode of epochal revolution, even though it may apparently be timed to appear in the wake of one such revolution in human society. The Book belongs to the era immediately to follow the conclusion of the present ideological struggle. That will be the day when men will be willing to seek truth and righteousness. When the chaos of the present confusion has passed, it will be more readily possible to formulate the cosmos of a new and improved era of human relationships. And it is for this better order of affairs on earth that the book has been made ready.

"But the publication of the book has not been postponed to that (possibly) somewhat remote date. An early publication of the book has been provided so that it may be in hand for the training of leaders and teachers. Its presence is also required to engage the attention of persons of means who may be thus led to provide funds for translation into other languages."

Upon receipt of these instructions, the Contact Commissioners entered upon the task of publishing *The Urantia Book* and preparation of plans for its distribution.

The Papers were published just as we received them. The Contact Commissioners had no editorial authority. Our job was limited to "spelling, capitalization, and punctuation."

Before the passing of Dr. Lena K. Sadler in August, 1939 she had collected about twenty thousand dollars for the publication fund, and these funds were used to set type and prepare plates for the printing of the book.

The Urantia Foundation

It was these plates of *The Urantia Book* that constituted the basis for the formation of the Urantia Foundation. This Foundation, set up under the laws of Illinois, was completed on January 11, 1950. The first Board of Trustees were:

William M. Hales, President
William S. Sadler, Jr., Vice President
Emma L. Christensen, Secretary
Wilfred C. Kellogg, Treasurer
Edith Cook, Assistant Secretary

It was learned that one of the wealthy members of the Forum desired to contribute fifty thousand dollars for the publication of the Book. By instruction, this was circumvented, because, they told us, it was best to give all parties concerned an opportunity to contribute to the publication fund. Accordingly, an appeal was made for $50,000 to defray the expense of printing ten thousand copies. The response was immediate. The sum contributed was in excess of forty-nine thousand dollars. The first money to reach the Foundation office was one thousand dollars from the late Sir Hubert Wilkins, the arctic explorer. The Book was published under international copyright October 12, 1955.

The Urantia Brotherhood

It was inevitable that some sort of fraternal organization would grow out of the teachings of *The Urantia Book*. All interested persons could see that the Urantia teachings were opposed to the sectarianism of Christian believers. It was clear that it was not the purpose of the Urantia Revelation to start a new church.

Accordingly, on January 2, 1955, a group of persons who believed the teachings of the Book and who were interested in their proclamation, assembled in Chicago and completed the organization of the Urantia Brotherhood, a voluntary and fraternal organization of Urantia believers. This group composed the charter membership of the Urantia Brotherhood, and were 36 in number.

A Constitution and by-laws were adopted, and since that date numerous Societies have been formed throughout the United States.

Distribution of *The Urantia Book*

At the time of the publication of *The Urantia Book* we were given many suggestions respecting the methods we should employ in the work of its distribution. These instructions may be summarized as follows:

1. Study the methods employed by Jesus in introducing his work on earth. Note how quietly he worked at first: So often after even a miracle, he would admonish the recipient of his ministry, saying: "Tell no man what has happened to you."

2. We were advised to avoid all efforts to achieve early and spectacular recognition.

3. During the first five years, these methods have been adhered to. The distribution increases yearly. At present, more than fifty bookstores, from coast to coast, carry the book.

The vast majority of the Brotherhood have concurred in this sort of quiet and gradual presentation of the book. Only a few individuals have exhibited some restlessness and craving for aggressive plans for increased distribution. One thing should be made clear: Nothing is done to interfere with the energetic and enthusiastic efforts of any individuals to introduce *The Urantia Book* to his varied contacts and human associations.

6

The Human Sources
and the Problem of Fallibility

Byron Belitsos

This chapter is excerpted and adapted from the author's book,
Truths About Evil, Sin, and the Demonic *(Wipf & Stock, 2023).*
It introduces the complex issue of the UB's *use of human sources.*

Numerous investigators have tried to determine who "wrote" *The Urantia Papers*. In recent times the federal courts may have settled this question after a decade of copyright litigation. In 2005 the Fifth Circuit Court of Appeals ruled that there is no evidence of human authorship of the text. Thereupon the *UB* quietly entered the public domain.

The prose of the *UB* is often sublime and inspiring. To many thousands of its readers, the text seems almost certain to be revelatory in a general sense. However, not every passage is by any means "inerrant revelation." In particular, the revelators tell us that the large amount of science and cosmology provided in the text is "not inspired."

And yet, compared to the utterly archaic cosmologies that accompany the Bible and other world scriptures, the *UB*'s "uninspired" sections on scientific topics are remarkable in their sophistication, usefulness, and consistency. These Papers play a heuristic role for readers searching for deeper meanings and values in a technologically advanced civilization.[6] At a minimum, the post-Einsteinian evolutionary cosmology of the Urantia revelation improves our grasp of faith because it inspires deeper devotion to our Creator—even as the *UB*'s statements about the physical world are slowly going out of date.

And yet, even with its self-imposed restrictions on revealing "unearned knowledge," much of the *UB*'s elucidations on cosmic evolution, physics, astrophysics, anthropology, geology, and biology remain ahead of its time even today—and some of its statements can rightly be considered "prophetic" as well as revelatory.

Equally important is the fact that the revelators brought to bear unusual literary techniques. Chapter 5 describes their plan for ongoing interaction with a closed group of hundreds of humans during the drafting process early in the twentieth century; in addition, they also had superhuman recourse to the best ideas of all humans in *all* fields of knowledge, deceased or living, in constructing the text. We are further told that the book's authors—acting in accord with their "revelation mandate"—were required to judiciously combine revealed knowledge with already acquired human knowledge, that is, their own selections of the most advanced *human* concepts known at the time. Most of these humanly sourced concepts express crucial ideas that remain pertinent today.

This revelatory method appears in part to have been designed to prevent the all-too-human-tendency to fetishize a purported "sacred text." It's worth quoting again: The revelators tell us in the Acknowledgement section of the Foreword that their charter was as follows:

> [To] give preference to the highest existing human concepts pertaining to the subjects to be presented. We may resort to pure revelation only when the concept of presentation has had no adequate previous expression by the human mind. . . . Accordingly, in making these presentations about God and his universe associates,

---

[6] See for example, "The Universe of Universes" (Paper 12); "Physical Aspects of the Local Universe," (Paper 41); and "Energy—Mind and Matter" (Paper 42).

we have selected as the basis of these Papers more than one thousand human concepts representing the highest and most advanced planetary knowledge of spiritual values and universe meanings. Wherein these human concepts, assembled from the God-knowing mortals of the past and the present, are inadequate to portray the truth as we are directed to reveal it, we will unhesitatingly supplement them, for this purpose drawing upon our own superior knowledge.[7]

In other words, the first three parts of the Urantia Revelation weave within its pages selections from more than one thousand human concepts that correlate and harmonize with the revealed knowledge that was mandated to be conveyed to humankind.

What, then, if our purported revelation—even as it appears to supply greater theological certainty, philosophic depth, and historic truth—also admits to its historicity, fallibility, deficiencies, omissions, and openness to revision in the future?

On the one hand, consider these points on the positive side. First, the *UB* appears to be both stunningly original and doctrinally definitive, and some of its factual scientific claims—unverified at the time of publication in 1955—have been validated by more recent discoveries.[8] *The Urantia Book* even asserts that "the historic facts and religious truths of this series of revelatory presentations will stand on the records of the ages to come." In the full text of this latter statement, the revelators contrast the *UB*'s reliability regarding history and religion against its own extensive coverage of the

---

[7] *The Urantia Book*, 0:12.11. This unique and sometimes baffling methodology is further explored in my book *Your Evolving Soul*.

[8] Certain researchers now point to what they regard as important subset of successes in this regard. Detailed reports covering these allegedly validated "facts and truths" have been produced by independent researcher and veteran *UB* student, Halbert Katzen, founder of UBtheNews.com. Katzen is a pioneer in this effort to reconcile the *UB*'s assertions with existing advances in knowledge.

physical sciences, which it admits will soon "stand in need of revision."[9] A major effort has been underway by *UB* students to evaluate the entirety of these "uninspired" claims, with some notable successes as well as failures.[10]

However, and on the other hand, we must now take into account the factor of human sources that are "fallible." As already stated, the *UB*'s superhuman authors forthrightly declare that they utilized hundreds of human sources, authors whose work had appeared in print up to the completion of the Papers in 1945. And, perforce, the revelators knew that many of these sources would soon become outdated. On my reading, such an approach is a built-in factor of self-correction that protects readers from the perils of dogmatic certainty and even text idolatry, even as these human sources provide frankly "imperfect" scaffolding that serves to support the book's purely revelatory teachings.

The *UB* provides two "Acknowledgments" regarding its human sources, but I cited only one of these previously.

1. As to the first, you'll recall that it made reference to "more than one thousand human concepts . . . assembled from the God-knowing mortals of the past and the present." This statement applies to the first three parts of the text.

---

[9] The following statement is the full text of this claim in the *UB*, with emphasis added: "Mankind should understand that we who participate in the revelation of truth are very rigorously limited by the instructions of our superiors. *We are not at liberty to anticipate the scientific discoveries of a thousand years*. Revelators must act in accordance with the instructions which form a part of the revelation mandate. We see no way of overcoming this difficulty, either now or at any future time. We full well know that, while the historic facts and religious truths of this series of revelatory presentations will stand on the records of the ages to come, *within a few short years many of our statements regarding the physical sciences will stand in need of revision in consequence of additional scientific developments and new discoveries*. These new developments we even now foresee, but we are forbidden to include such humanly undiscovered facts in the revelatory records" *(The Urantia Book, 101:4.2)*.

[10] A half-dozen formal events, known as "Scientific Symposiums," have convened since the 1980s. Many of the dozens of papers that have been presented are by authors with doctorates or advanced expertise in their fields. For the most recent event, see Scientific Symposium III, "Science: The Interface of Evolution and Revelation."

2. Its second "Acknowledgment" pertains to Part IV, "The Life and Teachings of Jesus." Here the revelators reveal that they made use of the thoughts of "more than two thousand human beings who have lived on earth from the days of Jesus down to the time of these revelations." Crucially, the chief celestial editor of Part IV goes on to state in this disclaimer that "my revelatory commission forbade me to resort to extrahuman sources of either information or expression until such a time as I could testify that I had failed in my efforts to find the required conceptual expression in purely human sources."[11]

Further, bear in mind that the text of Part IV was provided *as one completed whole* in 1934, thus obviously excluding the ideas of hundreds of prominent humans who have been writing, teaching, and preaching since then about the life and teachings of Jesus.

---

[11] Most of this second statement is quoted below, with emphasis added: *"Acknowledgment:* In carrying out my commission to restate the teachings and retell the doings of Jesus of Nazareth, I have drawn freely upon all sources of record and planetary information. . . *As far as possible I have derived my information from purely human sources. Only when such sources failed, have I resorted to those records which are superhuman.* When ideas and concepts of Jesus' life and teachings have been acceptably expressed by a human mind, I invariably gave preference to such apparently human thought patterns. Although I have sought to adjust the verbal expression the better to conform to our concept of the real meaning and the true import of the Master's life and teachings, *as far as possible, I have adhered to the actual human concept and thought pattern in all my narratives.* I well know that those concepts which have had origin in the human mind will prove more acceptable and helpful to all other human minds. . . . And when [such sources] of information proved inadequate, I have unhesitatingly resorted to the superplanetary sources of information. The memoranda which I have collected, and from which I have prepared this narrative of the life and teachings of Jesus—aside from the memory of the record of the Apostle Andrew—*embrace thought gems and superior concepts of Jesus' teachings assembled from more than two thousand human beings who have lived on earth from the days of Jesus* down to the time of the inditing of these revelations, more correctly restatements. The revelatory permission has been utilized only when the human record and human concepts failed to supply an adequate thought pattern. My revelatory commission forbade me to resort to extrahuman sources of either information or expression until such a time as I could testify that I had failed in my efforts to find the required conceptual expression in purely human sources" (*The Urantia Book*, 121:8.12).

Now, it had long been recognized that the Urantia text uses the Bible itself very extensively as a "human" source.[12] And it is evident to those who know their New Testament that the revelators "correct" or greatly amplify key passages (often doing both), addressing episodes from the four gospels in this manner. Plus, they add new episodes and introduce important persons lost to history who had interacted with Jesus. This includes the startling story of the twelve members of the Women's Evangelist Corps who were hand-picked by Jesus to complement the twelve male apostles, which is first introduced in Paper 150.

At this point, we are nowhere near identifying the "two thousand human beings" referred to in the second Acknowledgment. But researchers have to date identified over 125 books that were used as human sources for about 150 Papers (out of the grand total of 196). Notably, all of the known source-texts were published in English. The vast majority of the source authors were Americans or Britons writing in the late nineteenth or early twentieth centuries. Plus, they range across most disciplines.[13]

My own survey of the human sources used for the *UB*'s theology and philosophy of religion shows that the revelators draw heavily from post-Kantian liberal Protestant theology of the nineteenth and early twentieth centuries—or at least what was left of this movement (in the U.S. and the UK) after Karl Barth and his followers attempted to

---

[12] A reference created over several decades by Duane Faw called *The Paramony* provides over 60,000 cross-references internal to the Bible to passages in the text of the Urantia Revelation. A great deal more content is added to almost every detail of Jesus's life and sayings, but the Bible's account is clearly used as the "scaffolding" for the *UB*'s narration.

[13] The "*Urantia Book* source project" probably began in 1992 when independent scholar Matthew Block discovered a few books from the 1920s and early 1930s that contained close consecutive verbal parallels with various paragraphs in *The Urantia Book*. Block had been a student at the University of Chicago Divinity School when he discovered the *UB*.

dethrone the liberal Christian establishment in Europe using the cud-gel of Barth's *crisis theology*.[14]

We can speculate further that the *UB*'s revelators purposefully turned to liberal Christian thinkers outside the orbit of Germany, doing so for a number of reasons: First, the majority of the German church was about to capitulate to Hitler. Second, a sufficient num-ber of liberal American (or British) theologians had already trained in Germany or had been influenced by the post-Kantian tradition in other ways. Third, the ideas of this less doctrinaire lineage more closely match the tenets the *UB*'s authors had in mind and, at the same time, these thinkers represented the highest pinnacle of evolving Protes-tant thought—unencumbered by church authority—that had been achieved prior to World War II's conclusion. Finally, the *UB*'s revela-tors had obvious practical reasons for using English-speaking authors, thus obviating the need to translate such borrowed ideas into current English usage.

In this connection, we now know that some of the *UB*'s most notable source authors for theology were among the most respected American liberal theologians of the early twentieth century. The result is that the *UB* text itself communicates the optimism and self-con-fidence of that era that had survived in the academic settings of the new world previous to WWII's final horrors. Sadly, this mentality has not survived into our era of theology, which has had to confront the post-WWII horrors of the Holocaust and Hiroshima, nuclear weapons

---

[14] Historian of theology Gary Dorrien puts it this way: "Barth said liberal theology betrayed Christ by construing faith as a human work and reducing God to an aspect of the world process. Barthian 'crisis theology' was about the holy mystery and wrath of a Wholly Other God, beheld in faith and confessed in the language of paradox. Ritschl, Barth decided, was not worth refuting, having merely baptized the German bourgeois order. Harnack conferred scholarly prestige on Ritschlian theology. Tro-eltsch trivialized theology by reducing it to the ponderings of historicist onlookers. Schleiermacher was great, but also the beginning of the problem. Hegel was great, but Hegelian philosophy was a bad substitute for Christian revelation. According to Barth, Schleiermacher founded a bad approach to theology that led straight to the bankruptcy of of Ritschl, Harnack, and Troeltsch" (Dorrien, *In a Post-Hegelian Spirit*, 27).

proliferation, the advent of abusive technocracies, rising environmental devastation, and the gross failures of global governance.[15]

These American source authors include the likes of Rufus Jones, one of the most influential Quakers of the 20th century and Henry Nelson Wieman, arguably America's first Whitehead expert and a leading proponent of religious naturalism and empirical theology.[16] In addition, no less than Charles Hartshorne—a very prominent mid-century philosopher of religion—is also a prominent human source. Others include William Hocking, an influential Harvard philosopher who trained under idealist Josiah Royce and the prominent liberal Protestant theologian Albert C. Knudson, one of the founders of Boston personalism and a student of Bowdon Parker Bowne. Knudson was one among the "optimistic" liberal theologians who perhaps too hastily dismissed the gloomy doctrine of human depravity found in orthodox Christianity, according to historian Gary Dorrien:

> Explicitly, liberal theologians taught that animal beginnings gradually give way to moral endings. Implicitly, the upshot was that sin is a stage that can be outgrown. Nineteenth-century liberal

---

[15] The *UB* strongly commends the concept of democratic world federal government (see footnote 228), and it is fascinating to note that this largely forgotten idea was an important tenet held by what historian Gene Zubovich calls "Protestant globalists," whose heyday he says was the 1930s–1960s. This generation of elite American leaders assumed Protestant superiority in matters of ethics and morality, which led them to apply the principles of liberal theological tradition to a variety of areas of social engagement, including international relations. The social teachings of the *UB* reflect the optimism of this bygone mentality, and I have argued elsewhere that in some sense the *UB* is a species of Protestant globalism. See Gene Zubovich, *Before the Religious Right*.

[16] Wieman's 1930 book, *The Issues of Life*, is used as a basis for a section in the *UB* in which a philosopher at Alexandria reflects on his personal encounters with Jesus. According to Block, "the parallels [between Wieman and Rodan] shed light on a previously unappreciated dimension of *The Urantia Book*: the creative genius and spiritual artistry that went into adapting source texts for inclusion in the Papers. I am awed when I see how comments from relatively mundane books have been transformed by the writers of *The Urantia Book* into passages of great beauty and inspirational power." In 1930 Wieman was a professor at the University of Chicago Divinity School. For details, see the Matthew Block, "Rodan Parallels" and also Zechariah Mann's treatment of this subject in the next chapter. Note: It should be acknowledged, however, that Matthew Block has more recently moved on to a strongly deconstructive approach.

theologians took their animal beginnings very seriously, but the next generation of theologians believed that progress was advancing at a very rapid rate. The world was getting better; the power of disease was broken; American power and democracy were expanding; education was expelling the evils of ignorance; religious orthodoxy was dethroned; the kingdom of God was within reach. The rationale for straining out sin language was built into liberal rhetoric about it from the beginning. By the time that Knudson reiterated Bowne's position in 1933, minus the Victorian encumbrances, the backlash against liberal theology was devastating, shredding weak versions of it.[17]

And all of this makes one wonder: If the revelators were to return today, which of these erudite but overly optimistic thinkers would they carry forward as appropriate human sources for an updated edition? Which new writers would they add? Would they cite open theist, process, feminist, womanist, or queer theologians—or thought-leaders writing in other languages? Would liberation theology and social justice concerns become more central? What about drawing from post-Vatican II advances in Catholic thought? Which current theorists of religion, psychology, or anthropology would be cited? What new scientific discoveries would be referenced, including recent advances in astrophysics, neuroscience, evolutionary biology, and consciousness studies?

Further, in order to produce an updated version, would they once again convene a focus group that resembles the Forum that was convened in the 1920s and 1930s? If so, how might this group's composition differ from the white, Protestant, middle-class, Midwesterners who made up the original Forum?

The upshot is that the *UB*'s use of human sources as well as its mandate to adapt its message to the "thought patterns" (as the revelators call it) of ordinary Americans in the mid-twentieth century, gives us license to remain critical of the tone of certitude found in many *UB* passages.

---

17 Dorrien, *In a Post-Hegelian Spirit*, 215.

The Revelators Admit to Incomplete Knowledge and Omissions

It is also essential to point out that its alleged supernatural authors admit that there is much they don't know or understand. One of the best examples of such apophatic self-correction is found in this statement by a "Divine Counselor," a Trinity-origin being from the central universe who claims to represent (or actually "is") "the counsel of the Eternal Trinity." My emphasis is added.

> A being of my order is able to discover ultimate harmony and to detect far-reaching and profound co-ordination in the routine affairs of universe administration. Much that seems disjointed and haphazard to the mortal mind appears orderly and constructive to my understanding. *But there is very much going on in the universes that I do not fully comprehend.* . . . Notwithstanding my knowledge of the phenomena of the universes, *I am constantly confronted with cosmic reactions which I cannot fully fathom.*[18]

There exists a similar admission made by a revelator who is said to be a member of the highest teaching corps in our local universe. This author discloses that the calamity caused by the Lucifer Rebellion (covered especially in chapter 13) "had far-flung repercussions in administrative, intellectual, and social domains." After citing the many adverse effects, he confesses (with emphasis added): "*While we cannot fathom the wisdom that permits such catastrophes,* we can always discern the beneficial outworking of these local disturbances as they are reflected out upon the universe at large."[19] In other words, the wisdom that allows for this greatest of disasters remains unknowable to this superhuman author!

It is also notable that, in various passages, the celestial authors admit to leaving out certain facts and ideas they are not permitted to reveal because of our stage of evolution.

---

[18] *The Urantia Book*, 4:1.7.

[19] *The Urantia Book*, 67:7.8.

For these and many other reasons, it would be wrongheaded to think of the Urantia revelation (or any revelation) as the definitive source of all-encompassing explanations or to depict it as any sort of final truth or repository of indisputable information. There are no infallible scriptures and never will be, as this statement makes clear:

> But no revelation short of the attainment of the Universal Father can ever be complete. All other celestial ministrations are no more than partial, transient, and practically adapted to local conditions in time and space. While such admissions as this may possibly detract from the immediate force and authority of all revelations, the time has arrived on Urantia when it is advisable to make such frank statements, even at the risk of weakening the future influence and authority of this, the most recent of the revelations of truth to the mortal races of Urantia.[20]

In sum, a supposed revelatory text should not be regarded as too much more than a "heuristic" product that masterfully addresses current needs, thereby accelerating human evolution for a finite period of time thanks to its qualities of superhuman excellence. It may serve as an unmatched reference text and provide conceptual scaffolding for building a superior civilization, but no disclosure of the infinite, short of infinity itself, can ever be complete.[21]

---

[20] *The Urantia Book*, 94:2.

[21] Here's the complete statement I refer to in the paraphrase offered above: "These Papers differ from all previous revelations, for they are not the work of a single universe personality but a composite presentation by many beings. But no revelation short of the attainment of the Universal Father can ever be complete. All other celestial ministrations are no more than partial, transient, and practically adapted to local conditions in time and space. While such admissions as this may possibly detract from the immediate force and authority of all revelations, the time has arrived on Urantia when it is advisable to make such frank statements, even at the risk of weakening the future influence and authority of this, the most recent of the revelations of truth to the mortal races of Urantia" (*The Urantia Book*, 92:4.9).

7

"Revelatory Mouthpiecing"

Zechariah Mann, PhD (pseudonym)

Dr. Mann believes the revelators made creative use of passages from *Jesus and Ourselves* (1930), which was authored by a prominent liberal Methodist pastor named Leslie Weatherhead. Mann provides an original interpretative framework for understanding Weatherhead's book that greatly expands on various New Testament passages. Mann has taught theology at several major universities. He is a veteran *UB* student who currently serves as a Christian pastor.

Independent scholarship has revealed that Leslie Weatherhead's 1930 book, *Jesus and Ourselves*,[22] was used extensively as a human source in the composition of "Instructions for Teachers and Believers," an important teaching that appears at Paper 159, Section 3. (See its full text at Appendix A.)

I have coined a phrase for what the midwayers, the celestial authors of Part IV, seem to have done in that section; I call it "revelatory mouthpiecing." They have used a contemporary human author as their mouthpiece for a particular teaching session of Jesus that they want to get across to modern readers. This differs from simply borrowing and paraphrasing concepts selected from human sources for teaching purposes, as is clearly done throughout the so-called "religion papers" in the *UB* (Papers 99 to 103), for instance. With the procedure I call "mouthpiecing," by contrast, the words of the source author are

---

[22] Leslie D. Weatherhead, *Jesus and Ourselves: A Sequel to 'The Transforming Fellowship'* (London: Epworth, 1930).

attributed to a historic character, Jesus in this case. Because of this unique approach, we are forced to re-assess what we understand the revelators to be doing. It seems that they are not giving us a direct English translation of the actual words used by Jesus on that evening, but instead are re-shaping the words of a known twentieth-century author as their chosen vehicle. In effect, they are letting that author function as a mouthpiece for getting across the import and meaning of Jesus' original teaching.

Here are some examples from Paper 159.

At 159:3.2, Jesus says: "Never should a righteous cause be promoted by force." This is taken from "Jesus will not try to win even a righteous cause by force," in *Jesus and Ourselves*, page 28.

The advice to reject any "appeal to fear, pity, or mere sentiment" (159:3.2) is based on Jesus not using "an appeal to admiration, or pity, or fear," in *Jesus and Ourselves*, page 33.

The wonderful line "I will stop at nothing to restore self-respect to those who have lost it" (159:3.3) draws on the statement, "Jesus will stop at nothing to give a man back his self-respect," from Weatherhead, page 41.[23]

In fact, all of Section 3 draws upon Weatherhead, up through page 254 in his book, where we find a discussion about faith, fellowship, trials, troubles, happiness, and love.

If we take the revelatory claims of the *UB* seriously, we need to assess what this method of borrowing means. A few initial observations are easy to make, and would be hard to dispute, while some further reflections that I will make are more open to argument. First of all, we must recognize that the human sources are *major* contributors to the revelation; they are not just dipped into for a phrase here and there. Secondly, the use of these particular sources is not disguised but is highlighted, sometimes by utilizing chapter headings or quoting from the first page of a source book, as several researchers have shown. *We were meant to discover these books.*

---

[23] These and other parallels discussed here follow the findings of Matthew Block's research on Paper 159: https://urantiabooksources.com/wp-content/uploads/2020/04/159.pdf.

In this article, I want to focus more narrowly on what is involved in using a human source as a mouthpiece for a particular teaching session of Jesus. I would like to offer three alternatives regarding the historicity of that session and how it is reported to us in the *UB*: 1) that teaching session never happened; the *UB* authors have created a fictional teaching session in order to pour in some teaching content; 2) the *UB*'s re-shaping of Weatherhead's narrative really does capture the essence of Jesus' teaching that evening; 3) the *UB* version conveys some points made by Jesus that night, along with ideas that Jesus communicated at other times in his career, as well as ideas generated by believers over the centuries, including Weatherhead's own development of the same ideas. I consider number 3 the most likely probability.

In retelling the story of Jesus, the midwayer commission that authored Part IV made use of many authors, popular and academic. A midwayer writes: "As far as possible I have derived my information from purely human sources . . . As far as possible, I have adhered to the actual human concept and thought pattern in all my narratives . . . embrac[ing] thought gems and superior concepts of Jesus' teachings assembled from more than two thousand human beings who have lived on earth from the days of Jesus down to the time of the inditing of these revelations, more correctly restatements" (121:8.12–13).

The Truth-Stream

When truth is put into words, it is put into a succession. All truth, on the human level, is part of a truth-stream, a tradition. It may shock us to find out that the entire narrative of Part IV is not a direct translation of Jesus' actual words, that it is a reinterpretation, or even the reshaping of a series of interpretations, but that seems to be God's way—or at least the way God guides and inspires celestial revelators to operate. God always uses human conduits when it comes to communicating truth to humans. We may think of truth as "thought gems" (the phrase used in the quote above to refer to human source material), but it turns out that all these gems have been rolling along a streambed of tradition, getting their shine, their polish, from the human religionists whose lives they touched, and who then handed them on to a human author whose contemporary work gets utilized by the revelators. Each truth-morsel is a "restatement," a part of an age-old conversation.

All truth makes use of a truth-tradition. Biblical scholars know that Jesus constantly interpreted scripture. Scripture itself interpreted older portions of scripture, Ezra reinterpreted the Torah, and Jeremiah reinterpreted Micah. The *UB* lets us know of similar cases of restatement: Moses made use of the traditions of Melchizedek (96:5.3); Melchizedek based his commandments upon those of Eden and Dalamatia (93:4.6); and the Eden teachers re-stated the seven commandments of Dalamatia[24] (74:7.20). The *UB* revelators have plugged some new links into the "scriptural" truth-chain, using twentieth-century human authors to give voice to truths spoken by Jesus.

In the same way as they used Weatherhead, the midwayers used Harry Wieman's *The Issues of Life* as Rodan's mouthpiece in Papers 160 and 161, as has also been reported.[25] Rodan is identified as a Greek philosopher from Alexandria who had recently become a follower of Jesus through the teaching of a disciple who had conducted a mission at Alexandria. His story is unique to the *UB*. This beloved section of Part IV covers the art of living, first-hand religion, the lures of maturity and of committed marriage, and the effect of spiritual values.

Once again, three choices seem to be possible: Either Rodan is an invention of the *UB* authors; or their reshaping of Wieman's book is a faithful recounting of Rodan's teaching; or the *UB* uses Wieman to represent the main trend of Rodan's thought—but along with it come many of Wieman's specifically twentieth-century concerns and concepts.

Many of the topics covered by the figure of Rodan are also discussed by Wieman in his book, but the actual expressions we get are mostly those of Wieman. If we can accept that there are such things as "creature-kinship serials" (49:5), it should not be hard to imagine that

---

[24] See the entries under "Eden," "Melchizedek," and "Dalamatia" in the glossary.

[25] Papers 160 and 161 depict a series of conversations by apostles Nathaniel and Thomas with Rodan, who had become a disciple of Jesus. For the likely human source in this connection, see Henry Nelson Wieman, *The Issues of Life* (New York: Abingdon, 1930). See also https://urantiabooksources.com/wp-content/uploads/2019/07/160.pdf

a contemporary person may have truth-concerns that are closely "akin" to the concerns of someone who lived in the past.

Revelatory usage of *tradents* (people who hand on tradition) is nothing new. After all, Christians use the traditions handed on by Mark, Matthew (assisted by Isador), Luke, and John (assisted by Nathan) for the words of Jesus. The *UB* does so as well. It explains that Isador actually wrote the Gospel of Matthew and that Nathan actually wrote John, following the guidance of their apostolic teachers (see 121:8.5, 10). All four authors were gospel re-interpreters, or tradents. And of all the human sources used by the *UB* authors, by far the most important and most frequently used is the Bible. The four canonical gospels are the main source books behind Part IV.

Human Distortion?

We need to go on and ask ourselves whether the revelatory mandate to utilize human mouthpieces means that the revelation incorporates any distortions or biases from the human sources. We know that Jesus trained Peter and John and sent them out to preach, even though he knew they would not get it exactly right. The gospels incorporate some fallible human material, and the *UB* apparently does so as well—but not when it concerns the personal attitude of God! In that case, the revelatory author speaks authoritatively, and in his own voice, as does a Divine Counselor in "Erroneous Ideas of God," the last section in Paper 4, "God's Relation to the Universe." A Melchizedek does the same in the last section of Paper 98, "The Christian Religion," as do the midwayers in "Meaning of the Death on the Cross," at the end of Paper 188. They all vigorously refute any notion that salvation involved the Father being *persuaded* by the Son or by the Son's death. Rather, "the Father himself loves you" (2:5.2 and 180:6.8; John 16:27).

Nevertheless, it is a stunning discovery (to me, anyway) to find that the use of human tradents is so crucial that it is considered acceptable to allow the revelation to be heavily colored by the viewpoints of the human sources. The revelators *have* to use human mouthpieces: "The laws of revelation hamper us greatly" (101:4.1). This means that the revelation is flavored or slanted by some early twentieth century viewpoints, just as the biblical gospel was flavored and slanted by first century viewpoints. But again, when it comes to things of primary importance, like the attitude of the Father, the authors are crystal clear and without distortion.

Still, it seems that *UB* students need to have the experience that many Christians have had: the realization of the fallibility of our Scriptures: "nothing which human nature has touched can be regarded as infallible" (159:4.8).

Updating

Truths *must* be re-stated or updated in order to be influential. Luther's updating of Paul involved substantial distortion of Paul, re-shaping Paul in Luther's image, yet it was highly effective, and still shapes Protestant views about Paul. Similarly, Philo of Alexandria updated the message of Moses and made it accessible to many of his contemporaries, even though he hugely distorted Moses by making him sound like a Greek Stoic philosopher. Yet the *UB* repeatedly mentions Philo as an important teacher, barely taking notice of his distortions. Of course, the original Moses is probably unrecoverable. The Hebrew texts attributed to Moses are themselves the product of tradition and accretion, and wide scholarly consensus exists that they were written 400 to 600 years after Moses.

The *UB* actually draws attention to its updating process in an unprecedented way. For instance, consider their restatement of the so-called Urmia lectures, a formal presentation given by Jesus to religious leaders that is not represented in the New Testament accounts. This section, which is prefaced with the remark by the revelators that they will be "taking liberties," actually has Jesus talking about "the American Federal Union" (134:5.13) as well as calling for democratic federal world government! They revelators are virtually shouting at us: "Look, we are allowed to add present-day content to our narrative about ancient events." The America and world federation references are a red banner demanding that we re-think the way we understand this revelation. We need to recognize the process of updating, and the role that tradition plays in the transmission of truth.

Conclusion

By utilizing authors like Weatherhead and Wieman, the *UB* has salvaged a great liberal theological tradition that has since disappeared. On their own merits, these authors are worth reading. By leaving the fingerprints of some human authors upon the revelation in such an obvious manner, the revelators have given a clear message to us: "Learn that truth is conveyed through tradition; learn to dive into tradition and taste the truth that is there; read these authors! Step into the truth-stream!"

PART III
RELIGION, ETHICS, AND SPIRITUALITY

Prologue III:
Excerpts on the Restated Gospel of Jesus

66 And when the kingdom shall have come to its full fruition, be assured that the Father in heaven will not fail to visit you with an enlarged revelation of truth and an enhanced demonstration of righteousness. 99 *Jesus to the apostles on Mt. Olivet* (176:2.3)

———◆———

66 In preaching the gospel of the kingdom, you are simply teaching friendship with God. And this fellowship will appeal alike to men and women in that both will find that which most truly satisfies their characteristic longings and ideals. 99 (159:3.9)

———◆———

66 Simon Zelotes asked, 'But, Master, are *all* men the sons of God?' And Jesus answered: 'Yes, Simon, all men are the sons of God, and that is the good news you are going to proclaim.' 99 (140:10.7)

———◆———

66 Your message to the world shall be: Seek first the kingdom of God and his righteousness, and in finding these, all other things essential to eternal survival shall be secured therewith. . . .You are not to go hence in the proclamation of the kingdom, saying, 'it is here' or 'it is there,' for this kingdom of which you preach is God within you. 99 (140:5.1)

———◆———

66 Then said Jesus to Pilate: 'Do you not perceive that my kingdom is not of this world? If my kingdom were of this world, surely would my disciples fight that I should not be delivered into the hands of the Jews. My presence here before you in these bonds is sufficient to show all men that my kingdom is a spiritual dominion, even the brotherhood of men who, through faith and by love, have become the sons of God. And this salvation is for the gentile as well as for the Jew.' 99 (185:3.3)

66 No matter what blunders your fellow men make in their world management of today, in an age to come the gospel which I declare to you will rule this very world. The ultimate goal of human progress is the reverent recognition of the fatherhood of God and the loving materialization of the brotherhood of man. 99 (143:1.4)

66 John asked Jesus, 'Master, what is the kingdom of heaven?' And Jesus answered: 'The kingdom of heaven consists in these three essentials: first, recognition of the fact of the sovereignty of God; second, belief in the truth of sonship with God; and third, faith in the effectiveness of the supreme human desire to do the will of God—to be like God. And this is the good news of the gospel: that by faith every mortal may have all these essentials of salvation.' 99 (140:10.9)

66 Those who first seek to enter the kingdom, thus beginning to strive for a nobility of character like that of my Father, shall presently possess all else that is needful. But I say to you in all sincerity: Unless you seek entrance into the kingdom with the faith and trusting dependence of a little child, you shall in no wise gain admission. 99 (137:8.8)

ff Remember that you are commissioned to preach this gospel of the kingdom — the supreme desire to do the Father's will coupled with the supreme joy of the faith realization of sonship with God— and you must not allow anything to divert your devotion to this one duty. ™™ (178:1.11)

---

ff Jesus laid great emphasis upon what he called the two truths of first import in the teachings of the kingdom, and they are: the attainment of salvation by faith, and faith alone, associated with the revolutionary teaching of the attainment of human liberty through the sincere recognition of truth, "You shall know the truth, and the truth shall make you free." Jesus was the truth made manifest in the flesh, and he promised to send his Spirit of Truth into the hearts of all his children after his return to the Father in heaven. ™™ (141:7.6)

---

ff By the old way you seek to suppress, obey, and conform to the rules of living; by the new way you are first *transformed* by the Spirit of Truth and thereby strengthened in your inner soul by the constant spiritual renewing of your mind, and so are you endowed with the power of the certain and joyous performance of the gracious, acceptable, and perfect will of God. ™™ (143:2.4)

8

The First Two Beatitudes: The Bedrock of Attitudinal Transformation

F. Gard Jameson, PhD

F. Gard Jameson earned a PhD in comparative religion at Pacifica Graduate Institute in Santa Barbara, California and has taught Chinese and Indian philosophy at the University of Nevada at Las Vegas for two decades. This essay is adapted from his most recent book, *The Beatitudes: Explorations in the Attitude of the Soul* (Copper Canyon Press, 2022). In this brief excerpt, Jameson inducts us into the spiritual depths of the first two beatitudes as seen through the lens of a lifelong student of the Urantia revelation. He draws from the *UB*'s extensive commentary on these famous passages (at 140:5), which is preceded by many other clarifications and corrections (see 140:3–4). The biblical beatitudes are followed by the rich set of teachings known as the Sermon on the Mount (Matt 5:13–7:28), which are depicted as being given to "astonished crowds." But the revelators correct the historical record. They tell us that the beatitudes and Jesus's additional teachings were actually the Ordination Sermon for the twelve apostles given during a solemn private event held in "the highlands north of Capernaum." The Urantia text states: "The so-called 'Sermon on the Mount' is not the gospel of Jesus. It does contain much helpful instruction, but it was Jesus' ordination charge to the twelve apostles. It was the Master's personal commission to those who were to go on preaching the gospel and aspiring to represent him in the world of men even as he was so eloquently and perfectly representative of his Father" (140:4.1). Jameson does not concern himself with these purported historic facts, but instead plunges us into the deeper meanings of the beatitudes and encourages us to engage in daily contemplative practice in the light of their depiction of the proper attitudes of a follower of Jesus.

A s a professor of philosophy and religion for over 20 years, I have seen how my students are transformed by the attitudinal approach to spirituality portrayed in the eight *beatitudes* presented by Jesus at Matthew 5:3–12. These poetic passages open the Sermon on the Mount, the greatest homily ever preached. And everything that follows flows from the headwaters of these inspiring beatitudes. The culmination of this epochal sermon, too often overlooked, is the greatest of all invitations to transformation: "Be you perfect, even as your Father in Heaven in perfect," a teaching that amplifies the Jewish scripture: "Be you holy" (Matthew 5:48; Leviticus 20:7). This supreme commandment is an invitation to psychological healing and spiritual transfiguration, all made possible by a faith that follows from trust in the power of the bedrock spiritual attitudes previously cited by Jesus. In this essay we'll consider only the first two beatitudes, which serve as a rich introduction to the adventure of self-perfecting. My discussion in this essay also refers to pertinent passages in *The Urantia Book*.

You'll recall the first of the beatitudes: "Happy are the poor in spirit, the humble, for theirs are the treasures of the Kingdom of Heaven." Jesus is telling us here that the humble are rewarded with spiritual treasures. But what is really meant in this passage, and how does one recognize these rewards in daily experience? Many believe that Paul reveals and names them as the *fruits of the spirit* in this much-quoted passage at Galatians 5:22-23: "But the fruit of the spirit is love, joy, peace, forbearance, kindness, goodness, faithfulness, gentleness, and self-control."[26]

These fruits or gifts are clear indicators of character growth. In fact, when we meekly open ourselves to the divine presence and stretch ourselves to discern the divine will, we gradually and naturally begin to reflect God's own perfect character attributes. Such gifts don't easily manifest in those who are filled with pride, smugness, or trivial distractions, but rather in those who are both able and *willing* to open a space

---

[26] The Urantia revelation provides an updated list of these fruits in this excerpt from a post-resurrection sermon by Jesus: "Salvation is the free gift of God, but those who are born of the spirit will immediately begin to show forth the fruits of the spirit in loving service to their fellow creatures. And the fruits of the divine spirit which are yielded in the lives of spirit-born and God-knowing mortals are: loving service, unselfish devotion, courageous loyalty, sincere fairness, enlightened honesty, undying hope, confiding trust, merciful ministry, unfailing goodness, forgiving tolerance, and enduring peace" (193:2.2).

to receive the fruits of the spirit in mind and heart. These humble souls, once they recognize their human limitations, inwardly yearn to receive these treasures of the spirit.

This passage from *The Urantia Book* tells us that the reception of these treasures validates the truth of the gospel of love and delivers us beyond temporal difficulties.

> Such spirit-guided and divinely illuminated mortals, while they yet tread the lowly paths of toil and in human faithfulness perform the duties of their earthly assignments, have already begun to discern the lights of eternal life as they glimmer on the faraway shores of another world; already have they begun to comprehend the reality of that inspiring and comforting truth, "The kingdom of God is not meat and drink but righteousness, peace, and joy in the Holy Spirit." And throughout every trial and in the presence of every hardship, spirit-born souls are sustained by that hope which transcends all fear because the love of God is shed abroad in all hearts by the presence of the divine Spirit. (34:6.13)

Humility Always Comes First

And yet, too many of us are distracted by the *material* fruits of this life: wealth, fame, pleasure, and power. Such "worldly treasures" are unsustainable, transient, and insufficient to generate soul growth. By themselves, such selfish goals invariably result in *weeds of the spirit*: fear, anxiety, anger, impatience, paralysis of will, ill-will, doubt, and a lack of self-mastery. These negative emotional states obscure or entirely block the inner experience of the spirit. A person filled with worry, greed, or rage is incapable of joy or selfless service.

That's why, according to Jesus, humility before God is *the most important attitude*, coming first before all others. Indeed, being "poor in spirit" is the taproot and dominant theme of all the other attitudes. In the parable of the Pharisee and publican praying in the temple (Luke 18:9), the Pharisee is depicted as "rich in spirit"—egotistical, narcissistic, and self-referencing—but the publican feels weak in spirit, truly humble. According to the interpretation of this story in *The Urantia Book*, "One was self-sufficient, the other was teachable, and truth-seeking. The poor in spirit seek for goals of spiritual wealth—for God. And such seekers after truth do not have to wait for rewards in a distant future; they are rewarded *now*. They find the kingdom of heaven within their own hearts, and they experience such happiness *now*" (140:5.7).

Humility implies a distinct awareness of our many imperfections. We're not required here to feel humble around our human peers, but rather in relation to God's infinite love, endless mercy, and eternal perfection.[27] The only natural response to God's presence is therefore to bow in worshipful adoration and to enter into communion with the benevolent Indwelling Presence that is also the unlimited cosmic source of all things and beings. In fact, the deeper our communion with the divine, the greater our consciousness of humility and of vulnerability. Within such a sacred communion we are led to abandon any claims to self-sufficiency, self-aggrandizement, or independence from the divine source of life. We stand in a dependent relationship with God which results in an interdependent connection with our brothers and sisters, who are all sons and daughters of the same divine Father and Mother.

My own experience reveals that when I enter into contemplative communion, the enchanting presence of spirit becomes more apparent. God becomes more real and my own petty ego distractions become less real, much less interesting. The encounter yields a deep contentment and abiding feelings of joy and peace. And yet, I still yearn for "more," for something even more real. The Urantia text explains what drives this process: "Spiritual progress is predicated on intellectual recognition of *spiritual poverty* coupled with the self-consciousness

---

[27] "Jesus did not want simply to produce a *religious man,* a mortal wholly occupied with religious feelings and actuated only by spiritual impulses. Could you have had but one look at him, you would have known that Jesus was a real man of great experience in the things of this world. The teachings of Jesus in this respect have been grossly perverted and much misrepresented all down through the centuries of the Christian era; you have also held perverted ideas about the Master's meekness and humility. **What he aimed at in his life appears to have been a *superb self-respect.* He only advised man to humble himself that he might become truly exalted; what he really aimed at was true humility toward God**" (140:8.20).

of *perfection-hunger*, the desire to know God and be like him, the wholehearted purpose to do the will of the Father in heaven" (100:2.1).

The other significant source of humility comes from suffering, especially from trauma and humiliation. When we continue to experience the extent of our own weakness and susceptibility to error, we realize that humility is a very deep well! But humiliation can in fact be a great gift, forcing us to confront our egotistical inclinations. My own experience is that when I am brought to tears in the recognition of my own inadequacy in the face of the fullness of God's presence, I discover a way forward through the weeds of my own limitations to a more glorious meadow of love beyond.

Contemplative Practice Is Crucial

Seen in this light, the act of engaging in a regular contemplative practice is as critical as breathing or eating and is essential to attaining happiness. Without a contemplative practice, we are incapable of rising above our biological roots and our innate selfishness, an attitude motivated by animal fear. *With* a contemplative practice, we discover a quality of enchantment in our awareness; we begin to find purpose in the midst of apparent chaos—and we are motivated instead by love.

Contemplative practice opens us to commune with the inner divine source of power, wisdom, and compassion. Every wisdom tradition on the planet suggests that contemplative practice delivers us into that sacred silence that has the power to heal trauma and transform our moral character. These practices, each in their own way, lead to the humble surrender to a larger field of awareness that eventually becomes a nourishing field of unbroken communion. A helpful modern adaptation from these traditions is known as *centering prayer* (see www. contemplativeoutreach.org), a practice that entails four simple steps:

1. Choose a sacred word or your sacred breath as the symbol of *your intention to consent to the sacred presence and action within.*

2. Sitting comfortably and with your eyes closed, settle briefly into a quiet space and silently introduce the sacred word or

breath as the symbol of your consent to that sacred Presence and action within.

3. When engaged with your thoughts, return ever-so-gently to the sacred word or breath. Your thoughts include body sensations, feelings, images, and reflections.

4. At the end of the contemplative period, *remain in silence* with eyes closed for a couple of minutes. It is generally recommended to take at least twenty minutes for the entire practice.

Become Filled with Righteousness

"Happy are they who hunger and thirst for righteousness, for they shall be filled" (Matt 5:6). This equally inspiring second beatitude encourages us to cultivate an intimate relationship with the One who already knows everything we need. Our best role in relation to God is to surrender and pursue a state of unbroken communion. As we commune through prayer, meditation, and service, we catalyze our own transformation.

The second beatitude also suggests that we act upon the reality hypothesis that "righteousness" can be personally experienced, that a righteous character can be truly realized along with the ensuing happiness. The Sanskrit the root word *rta* is the source of our English word "righteousness." Its original meaning suggests that we live in a friendly universe in which divine order always abides, that is, a universal cosmic structure that is lawfully arranged. Further, these laws are the very fabric of reality; they govern the material, psychological, and spiritual dimensions of our lives. When we live in accordance with them, our life works. When we don't, it can't work! We suffer physically, mentally, and spiritually and may become the cause of suffering for others. The magnitude of suffering on the planet is clear evidence of our huge misunderstanding of the lawful nature of the cosmos in which we "live, move, and have our being" (Acts 17:28).

In this sense, true repentance is simply a return to living in accord with the eternal laws of life. These laws infuse the commandments of the various traditions, which in each case call for a deep ethical and moral awareness.

Hungering and thirsting are part of our daily regimen. We do not pass a day without food and water; we could not survive without these basic substances. Jesus suggests too that we can hardly survive without our daily spiritual nourishment. If we lack a reliable approach to such inward sustenance we become restless, anxious, aimless, and unfulfilled. *With* a daily regimen of spiritual sustenance, we garner the energy, the compassion, and the wisdom needed to be a force for good in this benighted and distressed world. Spiritual longing yields the gifts of wisdom and compassion plus an awareness of how to proceed.

How many of us fast, unknowingly, unconsciously, every day? How many of us go without a daily spiritual practice of gathering the resources needed for the day?

> It is most dangerous to knowingly engage in spiritual fasting in order to improve one's appetite for spiritual endowments. Physical fasting becomes dangerous after four or five days; one is apt to lose all desire for food. Prolonged fasting, either physical or spiritual, tends to destroy hunger. (140:5.8)

We might instead consider fasting from those distractions that keep us from our spiritual nourishment, including our preoccupation with self, wealth, social status, or personal achievements—every form of obsession with the empty material world and the shallow culture that surrounds us!

Contemplative practice stirs, stimulates, and sustains a desire for what is real and the ultimate quest for perfection. During our lifetime we are invited to advance through layers upon layers of superficial desires incapable of satisfying our holy curiosity and longing. Most of us are engaged in some level of addiction that diverts our attention from things divine. Those addictions only increase our frustrated desire for true reality.

This beatitude *assumes there is a divine reality, and invites us to act upon that assumption with mindful enthusiasm*, which is the very definition of faith. What we name that reality matters less than how we intentionally engage with it. In fact, this is a hypothesis that can be tested. Like a true scientific experiment, we can probe divine realities to personally discover their validity. All that is required is that we engage in the experiment as we would in a laboratory, with a quality of integrity and sincerity. As the inventor Thomas Edison engaged in many, many tests and experiments, so too we are called to test the hypothesis: God Is Love.

9

Philosophy of Living as a Path to Love: The Role of Truth, Beauty, and Goodness

George Russell, PhD (pseudonymous)

This essay by an anonymous professional philosopher is based on decades of study. It focuses on the UB*'s clarion call for a philosophically informed spirituality based on truth, beauty, and Golden Rule ethics.*

By our late teens or early twenties, we have begun to form convictions about what kind of world this is, develop responses to life situations, make significant decisions, and settle into certain patterns of action. For the most part, we are unconsciously weaving these ingredients of thinking, feeling, and doing into a personal philosophy of living—even if we don't call it that. Since our experience is a complex blend of cognitive, affective, and practical dimensions, we are hardly aware of what is going on.

But some of life's challenges force us to think and think hard. At some point we learn that our personal difficulties can be severe and are not isolated from wider issues we can't directly control. Whether we look at our individual lives or ponder where our planet seems to be heading, we may realize that desirable goals such as health, sanity, and happiness are in short supply for most people. We may at some point start searching, not for quick solutions, but for something solid, dependable, and wise.

To answer this need of today's seekers, significant resources are available in *The Urantia Book*. It sets forth concepts of truth to guide our thinking, ideas about beauty to attract our feelings, and teachings about goodness that direct our moral choices toward loving actions. In fact, the *UB* invites each of us to engage in a *project of constructing a philosophy of living* out of these many-sided concepts. This call is especially found in a remarkable statement we will examine in detail. It goes like this: "The religious challenge of this age is to those farseeing and forward-looking men and women of spiritual insight who will dare to construct a new and appealing philosophy of living out of the enlarged and exquisitely integrated modern concepts of cosmic truth, universe beauty, and divine goodness" (2:7:10). This grand endeavor, it is telling us, is not just *a* religious challenge, but *the* religious challenge of our age.

In what follows, I first explore the key passages that describe this project of constructing the new philosophy of living, add some specifics to the framework, and finally consider how this philosophy of living relates to today's urgent spiritual needs.

Exploring the Construction of the New Philosophy of Living

The author of Paper 2 describes this philosophy project in four robust paragraphs we will now discuss. We'll begin with the first paragraph, which covers the rise of secularism in relation to the one-sidedness of traditional religion, and then goes on to advocate that religions of the future give consideration to seven key themes based on the primary concepts of truth, beauty, and goodness.

> The great mistake of the Hebrew religion was its failure to associate the goodness of God with the factual truths of science and the appealing beauty of art. As civilization progressed, and since religion continued to pursue the same unwise course of overemphasizing the goodness of God to the relative exclusion of truth and neglect of beauty, there developed an increasing tendency for certain types of men to turn away from the abstract and dissociated concept of isolated goodness. The overstressed and isolated morality of modern religion, which fails to hold the devotion and loyalty of many twentieth-century men, would rehabilitate itself if, in

addition to its moral mandates, it would give equal consideration to the truths of science, philosophy, and spiritual experience, and to the beauties of the physical creation, the charm of intellectual art, and the grandeur of genuine character achievement. (2:7.9)

The first two sentences appear to describe the rise of modern secularism as a reaction to a religious narrowness originally rooted in Hebraic moralism. The result has been that modernity rejects the "abstract and dissociated concept of isolated goodness" inherited from this tradition. These strong words call out the "unwise course" pursued by the church and Western Judeo-Christian culture over many centuries.

The striking last sentence of this paragraph urges us instead to adopt a much wider embrace of values, one that also engages the religionist with various forms of truth and beauty. Such a courageous leap is what today's religion must do to "rehabilitate itself" and thereby respond to the modern secular revolt.

The full solution actually involves *seven* facets: In addition to the isolated theme of morality, six *new* themes should be given "equal consideration." These amount to three kinds of truth and three types of beauty. Giving them equal weight will place what were once understood as secular interests—such as the "charms of art" and the "truths of science"—in an uplifting and even sacred context right along with the valid pursuit of moral goodness.

The implication is clear. Religions of the future, if they are wise enough to give serious consideration to each of these seven elements of the ideal religious life, will emerge not as a limited and limiting part of life, but as guides to abundant life in its fullness.

The succeeding paragraph, quoted earlier, now offers us yet another bold leap. It calls for "new and righteous vision of morality," one that will promote the needed transformations of *both* secularism and religion.

Here the author calls for a more deliberate step: the construction of a "the new philosophy of living." It also explains that this new pursuit of the values of truth, beauty, and goodness can become "increasingly co-ordinated" in the God of love:

The religious challenge of this age is to those farseeing and for-ward-looking men and women of spiritual insight who will dare to construct a new and appealing philosophy of living out of the enlarged and exquisitely integrated modern concepts of cosmic truth, universe beauty, and divine goodness. Such a new and righteous vision of morality will attract all that is good in the mind of man and challenge that which is best in the human soul. Truth, beauty, and goodness are divine realities, and as man ascends the scale of spiritual living, these supreme qualities of the Eternal become increasingly co-ordinated and unified in God, who is love. (2:7.10)

But will this clarion call to construct a rich new philosophy of spiritual living appeal to today's rising generations? Over many years as a classroom instructor I have observed, to my dismay at first, that many young people were put off by the terms "truth," "beauty," and "goodness."[28] On the other hand, they welcomed words like "intuition" and "insight"; I also also found that phrases like "making a difference" and "giving back" communicated better than formal philosophic terminology. This youthful push-back seemed to fly in the face of the counsel of my professional colleagues who doubted the role of intuition in recognizing primary values or other key distinctions. Yet I met with surprising success when I simply encouraged students to begin with their own intuitions and go forward from there.

The Urantia Book dates from an earlier era, of course. While it hearkens to the old terminology with its roots in Plato, its phrasings are creative. It offers instructive variations that break through conceptual rigidity: God is said to be a "true, good, and beautiful personality" (1:5.2), and "God is the source and destiny of all that is good and beautiful and true" (130:2.7). We also find these restatements: "divine beauty, infinite goodness, and eternal truth" (180:5.9), and "truth, beauty, and holiness" (167:6.6). In another section we read: "Through

---

[28] In *Preaching as Poetry: Beauty, Goodness, and Truth in Every Sermon*, Paul Scott Wilson, professor of homiletics at the University of Toronto, uses other words for the values but still delivers the goods.

truth man attains beauty and by spiritual love ascends to goodness" (103:9.11).

Curiously, our second paragraph begins with a call for visionary volunteers. It is not an appeal to professionals. Those working on the construction project are to be, or become, "far-seeing and forward-looking men and women of spiritual insight." Intellectual ability may suffice for *gathering* concepts for the new philosophy. But to impact civilization, we are told that the project must *appeal* to large numbers of people, which in turn will happen especially when its proponents deeply believe in and *live* these values. This is why this project is called the *religious* challenge of this age.

Further, those who construct this new philosophy of life must also *dare* to do so; it takes courage to pioneer on these several fronts. Volunteers will need to seek out, study, and weave together "enlarged and exquisitely integrated modern concepts"—and yes, these more capacious ideas can indeed be found in *The Urantia Book*. But over decades I have learned that my own approach to the construction project, derived mainly from a lifetime of study of the *UB*, has been greatly enlarged by plunging into the work of other writers and testing their insights in my life.

The emerging philosophy of living we are encouraged to construct cannot be defined by a single text, as we see in this warning later in the *UB* text: "When you undertake the human formulation of divine truth," we are told, "it speedily dies" (180:5.2). Nevertheless, I believe our worldwide corps of volunteers will eventually harmonize their findings into a single emergent philosophy of living, one that lives and breathes. I believe this can occur because Jesus offers assurance that provision will always be made for "definite leadership" in the work of the kingdom: "In my universe and in my Father's universe of universes, our brethren-sons are dealt with as individuals in all their spiritual relations, but in all group relationships we unfailingly provide for definite leadership. Our kingdom is a realm of order, and where two or more will creatures act in co-operation, there is always provided the authority of leadership" (181:2.16).

It is well worth noting in this connection that the *UB*'s revelators, whose text was completed in the 1930s and 40s, will often use the word "men" to include women; but in this passage both are explicitly mentioned, which I regard as a significant emphasis. Future leadership in the great project will be shared by men and women working in partnership.

A few more comments on the sentences that conclude the second paragraph, beginning with the first: "Such a new and righteous vision of morality will attract all that is good in the mind of man and challenge that which is best in the human soul." *The Urantia Book* presents clear distinctions between body, mind, soul, and spirit (0:5.5-10); as we mature, we gradually get better at distinguishing them in our experience. Whereas we are told that the Indwelling Spirit is a literal part of God, the revelators declare that the soul is "the real you, your higher and advancing self, your better . . . future self" (108:6.6). Our soul is also "the self-reflective, truth-discerning, and spirit-perceiving" part of us (133:6.5). A person "experiences spiritual reality in the soul but becomes conscious of this experience in his mind" (103:6.6). "In so far as man's evolving . . . soul becomes permeated by truth, beauty, and goodness as the value-realization of God-consciousness, such a resultant being becomes indestructible" (111:3.7). Indeed, the creation of an immortalized human soul may be the ultimate purpose of the philosophy of living construction project.

And now on to the second and concluding statement of paragraph two: "Truth, beauty, and goodness are divine realities, and as man ascends the scale of spiritual living, these supreme qualities of the Eternal become increasingly co-ordinated and unified in God, who is love." In other words, many of the truths of spiritual experience engage with the love of God. Further, our encounter with divine love is the maximal possible experience of the beautiful. And finally, goodness and love are intimately connected; perhaps the best single definition of love, we are told in the *UB*, is "the desire to do good to others."[29] After all, God is ultimately the source of these three values and the highest

---

[29] Compare: "Love is the outworking of the divine and inner urge of life. It is founded on understanding, nurtured by unselfish service, and perfected in wisdom." (174:1.5)

example of each of them. They all lead to God, who is love; and the trio itself, we learn in the text, actually *adds up to love*.[30]

We started with seven themes, which were organized under our trio of primary values, all of which culminate in unifying love. However, we do not and cannot live our practical lives by means of such abstract lists. Instead, as demonstrated by my students, we live intuitively, in ways that are increasingly insightful and unified.[31]

If we lose touch with our intuitive grasps of truth, beauty, and goodness by plunging into explicit lists of values to be achieved, we defeat the purpose. And yet, intelligent work with lists such as those I present in this essay can also sharpen our intuitions; such thoroughness may enrich our path to the simplicity of love.

This philosophy of living is what I like to call *the long path to love*, a pathway always coordinated with the higher values through the vehicles of intuition and study. At the same time, this effort depends upon and draws from the *short path*—the immediate availability of love that is disclosed by God's spirit within, a love that gradually comes to dominate our relations with others. This short path may also be called the simple gospel of Jesus, which leads us to be reborn of the spirit.

In this light, it becomes more understandable that balanced growth in expressing the three values (in the course of engaging with the seven themes of the long path) is "coordinated and unified in God." This is made clear, I think, by the truth that our three supreme values are always found to be interwoven—as illustrated in the third paragraph, now up for examination. This paragraph not only covers the

---

[30] See 56:10.21 (this entire section is titled, "Truth, Beauty, and Goodness." See also 3.2.12; 5:4.6; and 140:8.31.

[31] Mind has three basic capacities for insightful intuition. The first needs a word of explanation; it is our mind's capacity to cope in the realm of nature with its cause-and-effect dynamics. "Matter-energy is recognized by the mathematical logic of the senses; mind-reason intuitively knows its moral duty; spirit-faith (worship) is the religion of the reality of spiritual experience. These three basic factors in reflective thinking may be unified and co-ordinated in personality development, or they may become disproportionate and virtually unrelated in their respective functions. But when they become unified, they produce a strong character consisting in the correlation of a factual science, a moral philosophy, and a genuine religious experience. And it is these three cosmic intuitions that give objective validity, reality, to man's experience in and with things, meanings, and values." (16:6.10)

phenomenon of interwoven values, but also their benefits and how to cultivate them:

> All truth—material, philosophic, or spiritual—is both beautiful and good. All real beauty—material art or spiritual symmetry— is both true and good. All genuine goodness—whether personal morality, social equity, or divine ministry—is equally true and beautiful. Health, sanity, and happiness are integrations of truth, beauty, and goodness as they are blended in human experience. Such levels of efficient living come about through the unification of energy systems, idea systems, and spirit systems.

I'm still working to understand this rich statement which offers even more instructive variations on the three primary values. It adds content to the new philosophy, conveys a promise of health, sanity, and happiness, and tells us how to achieve them. Along the way, numerous questions arise, but I'll address only a few in this short essay.

How, for example, can health be seen as an integration of truth, beauty, and goodness? First, because living in accord with the relevant truths of science is largely responsible for physical and mental health, and second, because beauty represents the feeling dimension of life, in which freedom from fear and anxiety has significant positive effects on the body and mind. And finally, participating in divine goodness by going out and doing good to others has well-documented health benefits.[32] The larger story of goodness is about—yes—the eventual progress of civilization, including deeply caring about others' health on a national or even global scale even as we care about our own. Such progress will bring about a great improvement in the health of the world's peoples.

And what is meant here by "spirit systems"? An example of a spirit system is the spirit of God within us, the Spirit of Truth poured out upon us all by Jesus, and the ministry of the Holy Spirit, including

---

[32] Stephen G. Post, founder of the Institute for Research on Unlimited Love, has edited *Altruism & Health: Perspectives from Empirical Research.*

the *spirit of worship*, a technical term introduced in the *UB*.[33] And we unify these systems by wholehearted decisions for the will of God; such decisions engage mind, spirit, and personality, which are also said to be unifiers.

Allow me to move on to the next and last paragraph in this series. This statement tells us about key functions of our trio of supreme values, gives a clarifying lesson on love, and provides perspective on the place of this philosophy of living in our ongoing education, which in turn helps us feel at home in an awesome universe.

> Truth is coherent, beauty attractive, goodness stabilizing. And when these values of that which is real are co-ordinated in personality experience, the result is a high order of love conditioned by wisdom and qualified by loyalty. The real purpose of all universe education is to effect the better co-ordination of the isolated child of the worlds with the larger realities of his expanding experience. Reality is finite on the human level, infinite and eternal on the higher and divine levels.

We might restate this demanding paragraph in this way: Let us not dwell in isolated or partial perspectives. It is far better to "co-ordinate" our lives with our holistic trio of highest values. This is the best course of action because it brings us in contact with "that which is real"— and it is by this method that we attain a "high order of love." Failure to fully embrace the primary values may instead yield conflict, even warfare. It may lead to what the text elsewhere calls "wars of mind and clashes of opinions" (25:3.12)—and may perhaps result in what we see before us in our era of polarization.

What does it mean here to say that "truth is coherent"? It denotes that, especially with a philosopher's help, the truths of science can be coordinated with the truths of spiritual experience. And what about

---

[33] Papers 8 and 9 set the stage for the ministry of the Holy Spirit as described in Paper 34. The spirit of worship is introduced at 36:5; but to understand it one needs to go to 16:6 for the discussion of our three basic insightful intuitions, causation, duty, and worship. In my experience, intuitive living comes (occasionally) as the fruit of working wholeheartedly and persistently with sections 2:5-7; 16:6, and 36:5.

beauty? Well, when we need a little vacation, beauty attracts the heart to sane and well-balanced pleasures, to laughter and recreation, rejoicing and awe. And finally, where evil tendencies may pose a threat, the stabilizing quality of goodness strengthens our hold on divine purpose and bolsters our trustworthiness in our relations with others each day.

When the three values are correlated in our experience, our lives are now "predicated on truth, sensitive to beauty, and dominated by goodness" (106:9.12), as we read much later in the text. Being "dominated by goodness" in this sense requires that we frequently commune with the divine spirit and wholeheartedly devote ourselves to living according to God's will, which leads us to love and forgive our brothers and sisters. And, because God's will for us as individuals is by definition in perfect harmony with God's will for everyone else, attaining a high order of love ensures that our affection for another person does not eclipse our loyalty to God and others.

Finally, what does this paragraph mean by "love conditioned by wisdom"? I believe it means that we rise to higher-order methods of loving others because we're in accord with the wisdom of the emerging philosophy of living. And all this is true because, as we read in Paper 2, "divine love functions in unified association with the divine wisdom" (2:5.10).[34]

Specific Paths of Ascent to Higher Levels

As we delve more deeply into the emerging philosophy of living, *two trios* may begin to stand out: our three supreme values plus three *levels* on which they are actualized, levels that can be generalized as "progress from the material, to the mental, and then to the spiritual."

Our initial sketch of the new philosophy becomes more concrete if we fill it out a bit with specific examples that account for our

---

[34] Here is the context of this quote from Paper 2: "But the love of God is an intelligent and farseeing parental affection. The divine love functions in unified association with divine wisdom and all other infinite characteristics of the perfect nature of the Universal Father. God is love, but love is not God. The greatest manifestation of the divine love for mortal beings is observed in the bestowal of the Thought Adjusters [the Indwelling Spirits], but your greatest revelation of the Father's love is seen in the bestowal life of his Son Michael [Jesus Christ] as he lived on earth the ideal spiritual life. It is the indwelling Adjuster who individualizes the love of God to each human soul."

aforementioned seven themes. At first we might consider these lists to be a staggering overload. But patience and deeper inquiry should reveal a rich set of resources for problem-solving that I call *walking in beauty*, *living the truth*, and *participating in divine goodness*.

Walking in beauty. As we progress in the affective dimension of our lives and experience the beauty of feeling things more deeply, we especially become more sensitive to others' feelings as well as our own; and we more often realize when a felt need arises that requires our compassionate attention. The Urantia text itself evokes a feeling relationship to the beauties of the physical creation, for example in this description what the 12-year-old Jesus saw while traveling with his parents from Nazareth to Jerusalem.

> The road now led immediately down into the tropical Jordan valley, and soon Jesus was to have exposed to his wondering gaze the crooked and ever-winding Jordan with its glistening and rippling waters as it flowed down toward the Dead Sea. They laid aside their outer garments as they journeyed south in this tropical valley, enjoying the luxurious fields of grain and the beautiful oleanders laden with their pink blossoms, while massive snow-capped Mount Hermon stood far to the north, in majesty looking down on the historic valley. A little over three hours' travel from opposite Scythopolis they came upon a bubbling spring, and here they camped for the night, out under the starlit heavens. (124:6.5)

Living the truth. Truth as depicted by the revelators has a spiritual core and a scientific periphery, and they make clear that these elements can be united by a philosophic bridge. Stated otherwise, truth is cosmic reality as discovered by scientific experiment and interpreted by wise philosophy, and whose essence is revealed by the spirit of God.[35] In this subsection, I will speak first of the truths of science, next of

---

[35] To speak of "cosmic truth" implies a synthesis of the truths of science, philosophy, and spiritual experience.

spiritual experience, and third of philosophy as the method for integrating the first two.

Here's a helpful way to frame this approach: multiple intuitions, with their threads of reasoning, are woven into wisdom. These same three elements (i.e., intuition, reason, wisdom) are characterized in Paper 101 as "spiritual intuition," "spiritual reason," and "the wisdom of spirit realities," (101:3.2). These are depicted in the passage as our three primary spiritual endowments. Here's the full quote, with emphasis added. I will allow you to draw any further inferences:

> Faith-insight, or **spiritual intuition**, is the endowment of the cosmic mind in association with the Thought Adjuster, which is the Father's gift to man. **Spiritual reason,** soul intelligence, is the endowment of the Holy Spirit, the Creative Spirit's gift to man. Spiritual philosophy, **the wisdom of spirit realities**, is the endowment of the Spirit of Truth, the combined gift of the bestowal Sons to the children of men. And the co-ordination and interassociation of these spirit endowments constitute man a spirit personality in potential destiny. (101:3.2)

For the daily practice of dealing with material things, we exercise the *intuitive* sensory level of the mind's three a priori discriminating powers (see 16:6.6, which is quoted in footnote 31). Accordingly, we perceive and then establish important empirical facts in our practical experience and may use *reason* in informal or even rigorous experiments to discover cause and effect relationships with regard to them.[36] At some point we can integrate the various scientific disciplines into what we might call scientific *wisdom*: a broad picture of cosmic evolution that encompasses such elements as biological evolution, personal growth, and historical progress.

In the realm of spiritual experience, one profound yet simple truth provided in the text teaches us how to ascend to union with God. "Man attains divine union by progressive reciprocal spiritual communion, by personality intercourse with the personal God, by increasingly

---

[36] *The Urantia Book* acknowledges the partial insight made available by reductionistic approaches (e.g., 36:6.1) but robustly challenges reductionism (e.g., 195:6-7).

attaining the divine nature through wholehearted and intelligent conformity to the divine will" (1:7.2). In other words, there is an interactive back-and-forth flow of attention and energy between God and us, and this intercourse gets better as we put what we receive into practice by doing God's will and then coming back for more, leading eventually to union.

Any such reference to the truths of spiritual experience raises many questions, especially how to sort out the true from the false in our encounters with what we believe are divine realities. Thankfully, the revelators assure us: "God answers man's prayer by giving him an expanded revelation of truth, an enhanced appreciation of beauty, and an augmented concept of goodness" (91:7.11).

But having given us this generalized assurance, the challenges that beset of human discernment are bluntly stated several times in different Papers:

> The [Indwelling Spirit of God] is engaged in a constant effort so to spiritualize your mind as to evolve your . . . soul; but you yourself are mostly unconscious of this inner ministry. You are quite incapable of distinguishing the product of your own material intellect from that of the conjoint activities of your soul and the [divine spirit]. (110:4.2)

> The human mind may perform in response to so-called inspiration when it is sensitive either to the uprisings of the subconscious or to the stimulus of the superconscious. In either case it appears to the individual that such augmentations of the content of consciousness are more or less foreign. (91:7.4)

Regarding discernment, my personal conclusion is that my responsibility in evaluating my religious experience is two-fold: (1) avoid making assumptions about the origin of any particular experience, in the knowledge that I cannot distinguish a top-down revelation from a bottom-up synthesis of the subconscious mind. With that in mind, my next task is (2) to reflect scientifically, philosophically, and religiously—that is, seek for the truth-beauty-and-goodness dimensions of a particular spiritual experience.

Let's imagine a case in which the subconscious mind has been working on some problem, in a process that was initiated because I have offered up a specific prayer.

I have found that the ideas or images that surface into awareness often come quite immediately to mind, and this response may offer considerable improvement over what I previously had in mind a minute earlier. I may even find this product to be true, beautiful, and good, which I regard as impressive. But this experience is not the equivalent to God himself providing a gift of timely revelatory insight regarding the situation I'm praying about. Long experience has taught me that discerning the will of God is not to hit an elusive divine bull's eye; rather, it is better to have a pragmatic goal: to hit a humanly accessible target that reveals to me my next step.

Extra help in striking this target comes from what I like to call a "levels-of-experience" list, one that rises from the material to the spiritual. The following list from Paper 91, "The Evolution of Prayer," provides a pragmatic test of response to a prayer or other forms of religious experience:

> The practical test of all these [apparent experiences of superhuman reality] is to observe whether these phenomena cause an individual:
>
> 1. To enjoy better and more complete physical health.
>
> 2. To function more efficiently and practically in his mental life.
>
> 3. More fully and joyfully to socialize his religious experience.
>
> 4. More completely to spiritualize his day-by-day living while faithfully discharging the commonplace duties of routine mortal existence.
>
> 5. To enhance his love for, and appreciation of, truth, beauty, and goodness.
>
> 6. To conserve currently recognized social, moral, ethical, and spiritual values.
>
> 7. To increase his spiritual insight—God-consciousness. (91:7.5-12)

How then would we define truth in this context, in the light of such a list of criteria? When the authors speak simply of truth (rather than "truths"), they generally refer to spiritual truth as a living and divine reality, and also as "coherent." God himself is "the life of truth" (5:4.2). Truth in this sense, I believe, implicitly contains truths of all three kinds we have considered. Analogously, it is said that in Jesus "were hidden all the treasures of wisdom and knowledge" 128:7.2 (quoting Colossians 2:3). Truth in its spiritual simplicity is described here.

> Divine truth is a spirit-discerned and living reality. Truth exists only on high spiritual levels of the realization of divinity and the consciousness of communion with God. You can know the truth, and you can live the truth; you can experience the growth of truth in the soul and enjoy the liberty of its enlightenment in the mind, but you cannot imprison truth in formulas, codes, creeds, or intellectual patterns of human conduct. When you undertake the human formulation of divine truth, it speedily dies. The post-mortem salvage of imprisoned truth, even at best, can eventuate only in the realization of a peculiar form of intellectualized glorified wisdom. Static truth is dead truth, and only dead truth can be held as a theory. Living truth is dynamic and can enjoy only an experiential existence in the human mind. (180:5.2)

Living truth is not a vague, abstract idea. It is an interior gift that illuminates the particular situation in which the recipient(s) finds themselves. Said Jesus: "Discern the truth clearly. Live the righteous life fearlessly" (140:3.18). In other words, frequently ask yourself: What is the truth, here and now? If the response is clearly given and pertinent to the situation at hand, then live fearlessly according to this discovery. But again, this is a high ideal that we aim toward without the assurance that God himself has literally conveyed such illuminating truth directly to us.

At this point let us shift into philosophy as the method for the holistic integration of these principles of scientific and spiritual truth.[37]

In a remarkable passage in Paper 155, Jesus himself teaches such an advanced philosophic method to the apostles. He calls it "truth-coordination." Here we are surprised to learn of a "righteous" method for overcoming a "one-sided" approach to problems, which Jesus contrasts with the narrow-minded thinking of his enemies, the Pharisees. He calls it "the beautiful wholeness of righteousness," and proclaims that if the apostles will only follow this "truth-coordinated" method, others will find this holistic approach attractive. In this unique sermon, Jesus gives the apostles a lesson about two levels of truth; the philosophical or "co-ordinated" level is the one his hearers are not ready for.

> In all that you do, become not one-sided and overspecialized. The Pharisees who seek our destruction verily think they are doing God's service. They have become so narrowed by tradition that they are blinded by prejudice and hardened by fear. Consider the Greeks, who have a science without religion, while the Jews have a religion without science. And when men become thus misled into accepting a narrow and confused disintegration of truth, their only hope of salvation is to become truth-co-ordinated—converted.

> Let me emphatically state this eternal truth: If you, by truth-co-ordination, learn to exemplify in your lives this beautiful wholeness of righteousness, your fellow men will then seek after you that they may gain what you have so acquired. The measure wherewith truth seekers are drawn to you represents the measure of your truth endowment, your righteousness. The extent to which you have to go with your message to the people is, in a way, the measure of your failure to live the whole or righteous life, the truth-co-ordinated life. (155:1.4-5)

---

[37] Other statements regarding integral synthesis are found, for example in 101:2 and 5; 102:2.5-6; 102:3; 103:6-7; and 103:9.6-12. A widely prized collection of wise sayings is found in 48:7.

When we strive in this sense for truth-coordination, we find the essence of a method for making moral decisions based on a replete concept of reality, as described in this earlier passage from Paper 101.

Science deals with *facts;* religion is concerned only with *values.* Through enlightened philosophy the mind endeavors to unite the meanings of both facts and values, thereby arriving at a concept of complete *reality.* (101:5.2)

Participating in divine goodness: When they describe the realm of moral goodness, the revelators provide a sequence of six levels of interpretation of the Golden Rule that they call "the rule of living." This rule covers the levels that may apply or be invoked when we do to others as we want others to do to us (see 147:4).

We learn of these increasingly truthful levels of interpretation when the apostle Nathaniel poses to Jesus the question of how to answer a man who wants to commit adultery with his neighbor's wife and appeals to this rule to persuade her. The reply by Jesus begins by laying out the first level:

1. *The level of the flesh.* Such a purely selfish and lustful interpretation would be well exemplified by the supposition of your question.

However, we should not imagine that Jesus thought that the body was evil. He adds:

You know that men are all too often led into temptation by the urge of their own selfishness and by the impulses of their animal natures. When you are in this way tempted, I admonish you that, while you recognize temptation honestly and sincerely for just what it is, you intelligently redirect the energies of spirit, mind, and body, which are seeking expression, into higher channels and toward more idealistic goals. In this way may you transform your temptations into the highest types of uplifting mortal ministry while you almost wholly avoid these wasteful and weakening conflicts between the animal and spiritual natures. (156:5.4)

In other words, the energies of spirit, mind, and body are all just fine; they simply need to be properly configured. Reinforcing this point, we are told elsewhere that Jesus's prayer life included "the mighty mobilization of the combined soul powers to withstand all human tendencies toward selfishness, evil, and sin" (see 196:0.10.)

Now on to the next level:

2. *The level of the feelings.* This plane is one level higher than that of the flesh and implies that sympathy and pity would enhance one's interpretation of this rule of living.

Sympathy and pity may seem mediocre, but Jesus had a tremendous capacity for these feelings. For humankind to live the rule on this level would immediately transform the planet. Putting oneself feelingly in the other person's situation facilitates sympathetic understanding and promotes identifying their needs. On the other hand, the higher levels of golden-rule living may limit the expression of this aspect of the rule, as there are other elements that must be coordinated.

3. *The level of mind.* Now come into action the reason of mind and the intelligence of experience. Good judgment dictates that such a rule of living should be interpreted in consonance with the highest idealism embodied in the nobility of profound self-respect.

I interpret this level to mean that we should live in accord with the truths of science to a reasonable degree. We can also live out the truths of philosophy—insofar as this is possible. In addition, we can integrate these insights of the reasoning mind with the lessons intelligently drawn from life experience. To treat others in the light of these ideals gives rise to the nobility of profound self-respect, which in turn begets superb respect for the other.

4. *The level of brotherly love.* Still higher is discovered the level of unselfish devotion to the welfare of one's fellows. On this higher plane of wholehearted social service growing out of the consciousness of the fatherhood of God and the consequent recognition of the brotherhood of man, there is discovered a

new and far more beautiful interpretation of this basic rule of life.

The authors used the phrase "brotherhood of man" to refer to a living and evolving spiritual reality. Today it's best of course to call it "the siblinghood of humankind."[38] The point is to realize and strive to actualize it. In this sequence, love begins to get real on level 4. Our life is to be dedicated to helping humankind as we are able. Our dominant motivation is love, the love of siblings. We love them not because we expect our love, friendship, and service to be reciprocated, but because others are children of God, divinely created, infinitely loved, with the spirit of God within them, endowed with free-will, and each one having to deal with their share of personal, local, and even planetary problems.

5. *The moral level.* And then when you attain true philosophic levels of interpretation, when you have real insight into the *rightness* and *wrongness* of things, when you perceive the eternal fitness of human relationships, you will begin to view such a problem of interpretation as you would imagine a high-minded, idealistic, wise, and impartial third person would so view and interpret such an injunction as applied to your personal problems of adjustment to your life situations.

The descriptions of these levels makes it clear that they form a developmental sequence; we cannot skip any of these steps. This implies that living on level 5, the moral level, with its "true philosophic levels of

---

[38] *The Urantia Book* upholds the truth of the fatherhood of God while affirming: "The name he is given is of little importance; the significant thing is that you should know him and aspire to be like him. Your prophets of old truly called him 'the everlasting God' and referred to him as the one who 'inhabits eternity.'" 1:1.6 (23.3) Our religious and theological language must always adapt to changing needs, as conveyed in this statement toward the end of the *UB*: 194:2.1 (2060.6) Jesus' message, as he preached it and lived it in his day, was an effective solvent for man's spiritual difficulties in that day of its statement. And now that he has personally left the world, he sends in his place his Spirit of Truth, who is designed to live in man and, for each new generation, to restate the Jesus message so that every new group of mortals to appear upon the face of the earth shall have a new and up-to-date version of the gospel, just such personal enlightenment and group guidance as will prove to be an effective solvent for man's ever-new and varied spiritual difficulties.

interpretation" and its insights and deep perception, is accessible only on the basis of dedicating oneself to the previous level, loving service of the family of God, as well as mastering the three earlier levels as well.

In the above quote, what is meant by perceiving "the eternal fitness of relationships"? Here are two moral mandates that are the simplest examples of this phrase I know of:

1.   Always to show adequate respect for the experience and endowments of their seniors and superiors.

2.   Always to be considerate of the limitations and inexperience of their juniors and subordinates. (107:3.4-5)

Finally we turn to level 6 of the golden rule:

6.   *The spiritual level.* And then last, but greatest of all, we attain the level of spirit insight and spiritual interpretation which impels us to recognize in this rule of life the divine command to treat all men as we conceive God would treat them. That is the universe ideal of human relationships. And this is your attitude toward all such problems when your supreme desire is ever to do the Father's will. I would, therefore, that you should do to all men that which you know I would do to them in like circumstances.

In my experience, it is easier to focus on theory than on the concrete and sometimes painful issues faced in the moment of encounter with the other person whom we are to respect, love, and serve. Therefore, whenever we receive new insight regarding a situation, we do well to put it into practice promptly before the moment passes. Nevertheless, "every step you take must be one of willingness, intelligent and cheerful co-operation" (34:6.11)

And now another problem arises: how do we know what level we are on? Levels 3-6 are packed with ideals that could keep us busy for more than a lifetime. My answer is that when we reliably satisfy a level description to a reasonable degree, then we are ready to put our main growth energies onto the next level. In addition, and as previously noted, in order to maintain our status on a given level, we will occasionally need to pay attention to the disciplines of lower levels. And we can also learn something by studying higher levels.

Allow me then to conclude this entire discussion by drawing upon this series of depictions of the perfect character of Jesus. Each one speaks for itself.

> Although the average mortal of Urantia cannot hope to attain the high perfection of character which Jesus of Nazareth acquired while sojourning in the flesh, it is altogether possible for every mortal believer to develop a strong and unified personality along the perfected lines of the Jesus personality. The unique feature of the Master's personality was not so much its perfection as its symmetry, its exquisite and balanced unification. (100:7.1)

> Jesus was consistently cheerful, notwithstanding he sometimes drank deeply of the cup of human sorrow. He fearlessly faced the realities of existence, yet was he filled with enthusiasm for the gospel of the kingdom. But he controlled his enthusiasm; it never controlled him. (100:7.12)

> Jesus was the perfectly unified human personality. And today, as in Galilee, he continues to unify mortal experience and to co-ordinate human endeavors. He unifies life, ennobles character, and simplifies experience. He enters the human mind to elevate, transform, and transfigure it. It is literally true: "If any man has Christ Jesus within him, he is a new creature; old things are passing away; behold, all things are becoming new." (100:7.18)

Bibliography

Post, Stephen G. *Altruism & Health: Perspectives from Empirical Research*. New York: Oxford University Press, 2007.

The Urantia Book. Chicago: Urantia Foundation, 1955.

Wilson, Paul Scott. *Preaching as Poetry: Beauty, Goodness, and Truth in Every Sermon* Nashville, Tennessee: Abingdon Press, 2014.

10

The Grand Cosmos: A Universal Theater for Soul Evolution

Byron Belitsos

This essay adapted from Your Evolving Soul *(2017) introduces
the* UB's *teachings about soul growth in the light
of the book's cosmology and theology.*

This is my belief: *The Urantia Book* provides an unprecedented disclosure of universe realities, offered as a cosmic backdrop for its advanced revelations about soul evolution and our eternal afterlife. The angelic and super-angelic personalities it describes are always at our service as supporters for our soul's progress and our efforts at self-perfecting. Yet, a cursory look at the *UB*'s catalog of higher beings can be bewildering. I think it is fair to wonder why the text must go so far with its long lists of odd-sounding beings who carry out so many strange duties. Is this terminology the signature of yet another obscure channeled tome destined to be ignored on dusty bookshelves? Or is this really what it takes to understand our soul's birth on this world and its eternal destiny?

Be patient, dear reader—for it all depends on one's premise.

The Personal Heart of Cosmic Reality

For some esotericists, the supreme organizing principle of the cosmos is *energy*; for others, *unity* or *nonduality*; still others, *mind* or *consciousness* is the key; and for certain others, it's *evolution*. But for the Urantia revelation, the supreme premise is personhood. The *centrality of personality* is the surprising core of this teaching, to which we now turn. In any situation whatever, human or divine, we learn from the revelators that the *personalities* involved are by far the most precious factor. "Everything nonspiritual in human experience, excepting personality, is a means to an end. Every true relationship of mortal man with other persons—human or divine—is an end in itself" (112:2.8).

In other words, *the reality of the personal* is—at any level and in any dimension—the most vital element of the wide cosmos. The *personal* is the point.

In this connection we read that "the universe is mind made and personality managed (1:6.7). The word "God" in this context denotes Creator deities of Paradise origin who create all things and beings in their local universe. Deity in this sense *personally* sets in motion the impersonal laws of nature and then oversees and manages the outworking of every facet of evolutionary reality, including soul evolution, doing so through their co-ordinate and subordinate deity associates along with lesser celestial assistants—all of whom are themselves unique personalities.

For example, single-celled life is formulated and then planted on newly habitable planets by specialized personal beings known as "Life Carriers," who go on to carefully oversee and condition biological evolution over billions of years. (Paper 36 is entirely devoted to their story.) Another example: The lawful physical evolution of stars and galaxies is planned and catalyzed by special supervising personalities—something like "cosmic astral engineers." This specialized corps of beings are, like the Life Carriers, revealed for the first time in the Urantia text. (See Paper 29, "The Universe Power Directors.")

We're told in the *UB* that energy, mind, soul, consciousness, evolution, and even spirit are subordinate to that which is personal. They all function, teaches the *UB*, in service to the dignity of personality, which is "superordinate" in relation to all these factors. And as a result, it would be fair the call the Urantia revelation a "personalist" teaching, in line with the contemporary philosophic movement known as "personalism."[39]

What, then, is generally meant in the *UB* by having the status of personhood? The first point to bear in mind is that book's definition of personality diverges greatly from that of today's psychology, which regards personality more or less as "observable human behavior." But according to the revelators, each of us has a God-given personality, a "fractal" of deity if you will, that is absolutely unique in eternity and most importantly, *unchanging*. All other factors of self or soul change or evolve, but personality does not. "Throughout all . . . stages of evolutionary growth, there is one part of you that remains absolutely unaltered, and that is personality—permanence in the presence of change" (112.1).

And yet, we are also told in the *UB* that personality is somehow able to "host" our living reality and unify the attributes of our subjectivity, while also being the very source of will, creativity, and self-consciousness. Our unchanging personality is, paradoxically, the factual foundation of the objective reality of our ever-changing human subjectivity.

To be a person is to enjoy an exclusive and singular perspective on reality that is singular in all universes. Personhood is that attribute of being that lets us exist as sovereigns in our own sphere of self-determination and creativity, allowing us to freely choose experiences, grow in knowledge and virtue, and evolve a personal soul that reflects every one of our decisions that have spiritual or "soul-making" import.

Of course, at the same time, each unique person is only one of a near-infinite number of other unique persons. All of us, angels and humans and even deities, share this divine endowment of personality, not as something we attain, but as a sheer gift that can remain *with* us and *as* us for an eternity (along with our eternally evolving soul, our Indwelling Spirit, and other attributes). Most significantly, being a person permits us to recognize and love other persons as

---

[39] According to the online Stanford Encyclopedia of Philosophy, "Personalism always underscores the centrality of the person as the primary locus of investigation for philosophical, theological, and humanistic studies. It is an approach or system of thought which regards or tends to regard the person as the ultimate explanatory, epistemological, ontological, and axiological principle of all reality."

equals—spontaneously so, and from the heart. Even after our transmutation in the resurrection halls of the afterlife, we will instantaneously recognize the personalities of loved ones we once knew on Earth. Why? Because this feature of their beingness is an unchanging and divinely bestowed reality, existentially supreme over all other factors of self, and inherently attractive and always cognizable.

To be a person is to be adorable by nature, lovable almost by reason of divine fiat; just behold any young child to confirm that truth. And that's why our Divine Parent cannot help but love each one of us, her children. Likewise, we can't help but fall in love with other persons once we get to know them over time. The glory of the originality of the idiosyncratic uniqueness of a free and living person is what arouses our love and affection for them.

If all this sounds too abstract, consider the lesson of Charles Dickens' story, "A Christmas Carol." Recall the scene when the Ghost of Christmas Present shows Ebenezer Scrooge a God's-eye view of the personalities of Tiny Tim, Bob Cratchit, and the rest of Cratchit's humble family joyously celebrating Christmas Day with what little they have. Scrooge suddenly understands them in the way that those on the other side of the veil always do, sees the error of his ways, and even falls in love with them.

Personality is both that which knows and loves and that which can be loved and known. Theologically speaking, we can say that divine personality is by definition absolute in its ability to know other persons and therefore infinite in its capacity to love them. The Urantia revelation (and most Christian theologians) teach that personhood is the central characteristic of God, who *is* absolute love personified. But the *UB* goes even further in its exaltation of the personal: "Personality is not simply an attribute of God. . . . Personality, in the supreme sense, is the revelation of God to the universe of universes" (1:5.13). As such, the "personalness" of Deity transcends God's other core characteristic, the teaching that God is pure spirit.

Think of God the Father as the absolute person. As infinite Father or Mother, he or she is the source and destiny of all personalities, and it is this Primal God who gifts us with personhood at some point after our conception in the womb.

Later in the child's development, the Father also confers on us a pure-spirit fragment as an additional and essential part of our self-system. This superb gift of an Indwelling Spirit carries along with it what I like to call a *soul-making function*: It confers on us the power to co-create with the Spirit—in its partnership with our own mind and will—an immortalizing soul, which our only true possession other than our personality and Indwelling Spirit. This growing entity resident in the higher mind is, if you will, the alchemical harvest of the memory-record of each important interaction or experience we have ever had. "Soul-making" means that each discrete record gets deposited *in and as* our growing soul. This evolving and ever-changing soul is yet another a separate and distinct features of our self-system.

Again, the personality portion of our selfhood is antecedent to and independent of our Spirit endowment and our soul evolution. In other words, for you and I, the component of personality in our self-system has logical (actually, *theological*) priority over the Indwelling Spirit and its companion evolving soul. And all this is the case because personhood is the source of sovereign free will as well as self-awareness.

If God is defined as infinite love personified, it follows that personality relationships of love and equality must be central to God's nature. God, the absolute Divine Person, is inherently relational, and yet is *One God* and *One Universal Power*. But how can God be unitary, self-determining, and self-subsisting, yet essentially loving and relational?

The *UB* asserts in its opening pages that all of reality and infinity emanate from three primal personalities, the Eternal Trinity—which are nonetheless perfectly and seamlessly unified in and as the "One Father." Again, how can this be?

> Divine personality is not self-centered; self-distribution and sharing of personality characterize divine freewill selfhood. Creatures crave association with other personal creatures; Creators are moved to share divinity with their universe children; the personality of the Infinite is disclosed as the Universal Father, who shares reality of being and equality of self with two co-ordinate personalities, the Eternal Son and the [Infinite Spirit]. (10:1.3)

In other words, God's ineluctable sharing of himself—her "fatherly and motherly" bestowal of selfhood on others—reveals the primal nature of personality for the ages. "There is inherent in the selfless, loving, and lovable nature of the Universal Father something which causes him to reserve to himself the exercise of only those powers and that authority which he apparently finds it impossible to delegate or to bestow" (10:1.1).

The sublime community of absolute beings that we call the Eternal Trinity is the result of the Father-Mother's desire to articulate and self-distribute his infinite love. Of course, this "sharing event" occurred in the eternity of the past, establishing thereby the pattern for *all* subsequent communities and families in all domains.

According to the authors of the Urantia text, it was a virtual philosophic miracle that the theologians of the early Christian church were able to establish—in broad outline—a generally *correct* doctrine of the Trinity, even in the face of a thousand years of Hebraic monotheism. I believe this was possible because of their proximity to the powerful historic reality of the life of Jesus, whose claim to be the literal Son of God—one in essence with the Father yet distinct from him—was accepted by the early Church against other plausible interpretations of his miraculous career.[40]

Neither Judaism nor Islam could accept the disruptive notion that the person of Jesus could be in any way the divine equivalent of the

---

[40] They achieved these theological heights because of the primary intuition of the Church Fathers who held that Jesus was "homoousius" (one in essence) with the Father, while also fully human. Led in particular in the fourth century by St. Athanasius of Alexandria, the Council of Nicaea (325) repudiated Arianism (the belief that God the Son is fundamentally inferior to God the Father). Instead, they adopted the view that Jesus as Son was "light from light, true God of true God," that is, ontologically equal to the Father. In addition, in Constantinople in 381, the Second Council spoke more clearly of the Holy Spirit as equal to the other two Persons, and should be "worshipped together with the Father and the Son." (This essential teaching of the equality of the Third Person of the Trinity is also affirmed and greatly expanded in *The Urantia Book*.) The *UB* singles out Athanasius in this passage: "It was a Greek, from Egypt, who so bravely stood up at Nicaea and so fearlessly challenged this assembly that it dared not so obscure the concept of the nature of Jesus that the real truth of his bestowal might have been in danger of being lost to the world. This Greek's name was Athanasius, and but for the eloquence and the logic of this believer, the persuasions of Arius would have triumphed" (130:0.18).

Creator Father, while also human. Both religions held firm to the idea of God's indivisibility and oneness—that is, their essential monotheistic doctrine that there can be no co-equal and coordinate deity called the Son of God or Spirit of God.

For example, perhaps Islam's most important belief about Allah (God) is summed up in the word *Tawhid*, the pristine notion of Allah's utter uniqueness. Tawhid teaches that God can have "no partners," no offspring that are equal in divinity. In Surah 112 we read: "He is Allah, the One and Only; Allah, the Eternal, Absolute; none is born of Him, nor is He born; And there is none like Him." No doubt about it, Muhammad's clear-cut monotheism offered a distinct advance over the polytheism of his contemporaries. His followers to their credit have consistently taught and celebrated this great truth of the oneness and unity of a personal God of love and mercy, uplifting and blessing innumerable souls over the centuries.

Trinitarians hold high this same concept of the One God and consider it a great truth, but only as *one* among *other* essential truths. Speaking alike to the "nondualist" mystic as well as to the monistic philosopher and the monotheist theologian, the *UB* asserts that the scope of the love and versatility of deity can be even greater than to merely radiate from a single universal center. The Urantia revelation as well as settled Christian doctrine stretches us with an equally important truth: the notion of God as *parental* at all levels, even *within* the Father's exclusive divine sphere of eternity, where the phenomenon of fatherhood (or parenthood) and sonship (or daughtership) first appears in cosmic reality—but of course, always bear in mind that gender is not literal at this level.

A self-existing God of no external relations of equality does not sound like a deity who would constitute a vast universe of creatures born into families of children with co-equal male and female parents. God as Father (and Mother) sets it all in motion, becoming the first parent in eternity. The Father and Son then unite outside of time to parent the *Infinite Spirit*, and these three (in different permutations known as "triodities" that is beyond the scope of this introductory essay) create and love all other living beings.

In other words, a loving Father who is the ultimate parent of a universal cosmic family must have his own "family of equals" that allows a replete expression of God's regard for other beings—thereby providing the archetypal pattern of human parentage and human relationships of love, friendship, and mutual regard.

And, more to the point of our inquiry: A loving and parental God would provide for our soul evolution by creating a rich array of divine agencies—some coordinate, and others subordinate—that nurture us from infancy to eventual perfection. The Urantia revelation explains in detail how the two other coordinate divine personalities, the Eternal Son and the Infinite Spirit, provide additional reality domains that become discrete platforms for specific ministries to us as their beloved creatures. The Son and the Spirit are genuinely co-equal *sources and centers* of true realities that are essential factors in soul growth and self-perfection.

11

The Urantia Book on the Apostle Paul: The Question of Mystery Cult Influence

Zechariah Mann, PhD (Pseudonym)

This essay showcases what exemplary UB *scholarship can look like. While this piece is longer than others in the anthology, such in-depth research is critical for illustrating how* The Urantia Book *builds upon and corrects ancient scripture. Mann points the way to future scholarship of this kind.*

According to Mann, the revelators "condemn" Paul's doctrine of atonement and are "quite negative" about some of Paul's theological compromises. The *UB* itself states: "Many of the great truths taught by Jesus were almost lost in these early compromises, but they yet slumber in this religion of paganized Christianity, which was in turn the Pauline version of the life and teachings of the Son of Man."[41] This research essay considers the *UB*'s depiction of the central role of Paul in the formation of Christian thought, with special reference to how it utilizes human authors who were critics of Paul. Mann situates these human sources within the context of biblical scholarship at the time the *UB* was written in the early decades of the twentieth century, arguing that the revelators sometime made surprising use of the most radical critics of Paul.

A note to those less interested in the details: Read part 1 to obtain a profitable overview of the *UB*'s fascinating take on the crucial legacy of Pauline Christianity.

---

[41] *UB* 195:0.18 (2070:14).

1. What *The Urantia Book* Says about Paul

The Urantia Book (hereafter "the *UB*" or "*UB*") states that Paul received special communications on some subjects, and was even granted a view of some of the "architectural worlds" (higher worlds made-to-order that we will encounter in the afterlife). The *UB* authors allow that he was a highly effective preacher and organizer, but they condemn his doctrine of atonement for implying that God was vengeful and had to be appeased. The midwayers are quite negative about some of his theological compromises, especially his (alleged) adaptation of salvation concepts from the mystery cult of the god Mithras.

The assertion that Paul altered the gospel so as to draw gentiles away from the mystery cults by offering them a better mystery, strikes to the heart of the legitimacy of his teachings, and has been a matter of heated controversy within biblical scholarship for over a hundred years. Currently, the idea does not enjoy much support among scholars, since there is no smoking gun, no hard evidence of such a connection. Assertions of mystery cult influence on Paul are now generally considered highly subjective and impossible to prove. I think Paul did indeed borrow some mystery cult imagery, but would never admit to doing so. What he admitted, and foregrounded, was Jewish theology. Mystery religions would be contemptible abominations, and he in fact seems to be insulting Mithraic initiatory rituals in Romans 1:21–25: "They exchanged the glory of the immortal God for images resembling a mortal human being or birds or four-footed animals or reptiles" (1:23).

My main pursuit in this essay will be to gather information about how the authors of the *UB* drew upon twentieth century scholarship when asserting mystery cult linkages. Part of my endeavor will be to locate the particular authors (the "human sources") utilized by the authors of the *UB* on this subject. But first I want to *situate* the human sources within the context of biblical scholarship at the time the *UB* was written down in English, in the early decades of the twentieth century. We have not answered any crucial questions if we merely identify the authors used, but ignore the authors *they* were using, that is, the trends of scholarship upon which the human sources were drawing. My method will enable us to see how the *UB* authors picked and chose from among the various currents of scholarship. What they did *not* use is as instructive as what they *did* use.

1.1 Liberal and Radical Scholarship

The human sources utilized in Parts III and IV of the *UB*, whether on religious history or theology, generally fit into the category of mainstream and liberal scholarship and theology, lines of thought developed by Albrecht Ritschl, Adolf von Harnack, William Hocking, John Baillie, and popular writers like Lewis Browne. The midwayers, in Part IV, make extensive use of a more conservative writer, a convert to evangelical Protestantism, Alfred Edersheim. What is surprising about *The Urantia Book's* angle on Paul, in particular, is how radical it is. When discussing any other religious subject, they consistently avoid the radicals, even when those authors are close to others whom they *do* utilize. For instance, the revelators use many concepts associated with the social gospel movement (especially the Fatherhood of God and Brotherhood of Man, but also the idea of the progressive development of religion), but they do not use the ideas or expressions of the most prominent social gospel writer, Walter Rauschenbusch, whose views were apparently too politicized and possibly too Marxian. Yet, in speaking of Paul, they are willing to use some of the most radical criticism of Christianity, possibly even that of the secularist Sir James Frazer.

I call it radical scholarship to distinguish it from the liberal scholarship that emphasized ethics and progress. What I am calling radical was the so-called "higher criticism" of the New Testament, first undertaken by F. C. Baur, W. Wrede and others, which was at the forefront of scholarship in its day. As this school developed, however, some of its representatives (Reitzenstein, for instance) were recognized as radical even by their contemporaries.

The old liberal type of scholarship is all but dead today, its optimism about human progress bearing the stamp of another age. Today there are many approaches, sometimes making use of archaeology, sociology, and literary criticism, as well as those disciplines that have always been essential for biblical scholarship: historical and linguistic knowledge. Some scholars have a decidedly left-wing stamp, some a strong commitment to evangelical viewpoints. The layman who wishes to look into this field can find many good introductory books on the subject. All books, however, bear the author's "slant"; the discerning reader must develop a technique for gathering and interpreting the material.

1.2 *Urantia Book* Views on Paul's Compromises

Almost all of the *UB*'s statements linking Paul to the imagery of the mystery cults, especially that of Mithras, occur in Part IV:

> Paul, in an effort to utilize the widespread adherence to the better types of the mystery religions, made certain adaptations of the teachings of Jesus so as to render them more acceptable to a larger number of prospective converts.[42]

> But Paul's theory of original sin, the doctrines of hereditary guilt and innate evil and redemption therefrom, was partially Mithraic in origin, having little in common with Hebrew theology, Philo's philosophy, or Jesus' teachings.[43]

> The gospel of Jesus, as it was embodied in Paul's cult of Antioch Christianity, became blended with the following teachings:

> 1. The philosophic reasoning of the Greek proselytes to Judaism, including some of their concepts of the eternal life.

> 2. The appealing teachings of the prevailing mystery cults, especially the Mithraic doctrines of redemption, atonement, and salvation by the sacrifice made by some god. 3. The sturdy morality of the established Jewish religion.[44]

---

[42] *UB* 121:5.13. This passage has no known human source.

[43] *UB* 121:6.5 (1339:1). Partly based on Alfred Edersheim, *The Life and Times of Jesus the Messiah*, Volume One (Eighth Edition; New York: Longmans, Green and Co., 1907), 52, which does not, however, mention Mithraism. This is on p. 36 in the still-in-print version by Hendrickson Publishers.

[44] *UB* 121:7.8 (1340:6-9). Compare 195:0 (2070:5), which refers to compromises made by "the Christian leaders." No known human source.

Aside from the incorporation of many teachings from the Persian mysteries and much of the Greek philosophy into early Christianity, two great mistakes were made:

1. The effort to connect the gospel teaching directly onto the Jewish theology, as illustrated by the Christian doctrines of the atonement—the teaching that Jesus was the sacrificed Son who would satisfy the Father's stern justice and appease the divine wrath. . . .

2. The second great blunder of the Master's early followers, and one which all subsequent generations have persisted in perpetuating, was to organize the Christian teaching so completely about the person of Jesus.[45]

Some of these passages draw on human sources, but they insert material about Mithraism that is not in the source. For instance, the quote above beginning, "But Paul's theory of original sin" draws on Edersheim, but the phrase "was partially Mithraic in origin" is not in Edersheim's book.[46] The midwayers are often quite harsh with Paul:

Many of the great truths taught by Jesus were almost lost in these early compromises, but they yet slumber in this religion of paganized Christianity, which was in turn the Pauline version of the life and teachings of the Son of Man.[47]

There is nothing along these lines in Part III, although there are many places where a linkage between Paul and the mysteries *could* have been made, especially in sections 98:4–6 that discuss the mystery cults. The most explicit passage I could find was one that sounds more like a hint than an assertion. The author mentions a number of influences that shaped Christianity, including Mithraism, and then refers to:

---

[45] *UB* 149:2.2-4 (1670:3-5). No known human source.

[46] Edersheim, *Life and Times of Jesus the Messiah*, 1:52. See https://urantiabook-sources.com/wp-content/uploads/2016/11/121.pdf.

[47] *UB* 195:0.18 (2070:14).

The personal viewpoint of Paul of Tarsus. And it should be recorded that Mithraism was the dominant religion of Tarsus during his adolescence.[48]

But this author also credits Paul with recognizing that Jesus did *not* come to earth "to reconcile an angry God."[49] He quotes 2 Cor 5:19 to make this point, a passage that contains atonement thinking, but which says that God was not *persuaded* to make reconciliation. The revelator quotes a Pauline atonement passage to point out something that Paul got right!

> A Creator Son did not incarnate in the likeness of mortal flesh and bestow himself upon the humanity of Urantia to reconcile an angry God but rather to win all mankind to the recognition of the Father's love and to the realization of their sonship with God. After all, even the great advocate of the atonement doctrine realized something of this truth, for he declared that "God was in Christ reconciling the world to himself."[50]

In other words, God was not being *persuaded* to do this, but was reconciling the world out of his own free will. What the revelators oppose is the idea that God was manipulated or appeased or persuaded in any way. The author goes out of his way to affirm a verse by Paul that shares this viewpoint, although he does *not* affirm the atonement idea that occurs two verses later: "For our sake he made him to be sin who knew no sin, so that in him we might become the righteousness of God" (2 Cor 5:21).

Compared to the boldness of the Midwayer Commission, the Melchizedek author of Paper 98 is reticent to blame Paul for mystery cult usage, though he does talk about *Christian* use of mystery concepts

---

[48] *UB* 98:7.9 (1084:8).

[49] *UB* 98:7.1 (1083:6).

[50] *UB* 98:7.1 (1083:6); and 2 Cor 5:19. The point is that Paul recognizes God was not *persuaded* in any way; God was acting upon God's own will.

and holy days.[51] Yet the most extensive discussion of Mithraism in the *UB* is in this paper (98). I am not going to say that this Melchizedek has a different *opinion* from the midwayers, but the important difference in emphasis must be noticed.

In the body of this study I will examine what biblical and anthropological scholars in the period before and during the delivery of the Urantia Papers were saying about the mystery cults and their possible relation to Paul's teachings. I will also cite the human source authors whom the Melchizedek uses in his remarks on Mithraism. In this way, we can situate the *UB*'s remarks on the mystery cults (in Parts 3 and 4) and on *Paul and* the mystery cults (in Part 4) within the field of then-contemporary scholarship.

But first I must make a brief diversion.

1.3 Misattribution of Hebrews to Paul

An intriguing "mistake" of some of the *UB* authors is their attribution of the Epistle to the Hebrews to Pauline authorship:

> And this is the origin of sacrifices as a part of worship. This idea was elaborated by Moses in the Hebrew ritual and was preserved, in principle, by the Apostle Paul as the doctrine of atonement for sin by "the shedding of blood."[52]

This refers to Heb 9:22: "under the law almost everything is purified with blood, and without the shedding of blood there is no forgiveness."

Another author attributes the passages in Heb 10:34; 11:10, 16 to Paul—and uses the King James translation for Heb 10:34 ("a better and more enduring substance"),[53] although the revelators usually use the ASV (American Standard Version) translation of the Bible.

And a third Part III author attributes Heb 12:22–23 ("to an innumerable company of angels") to Paul, although this author adds

---

[51] In *UB* 98:5–6 (1082:3–1083:5); specific quotes will be given in later sections.

[52] *UB* 63:6.4 (716:3). The author is a "Life Carrier," and is writing on an anthropological/historical, not a biblical, subject.

[53] *UB* 48:1.7 (542:4). The author is "an Archangel."

something that evidently was changed in the biblical text: "to the grand assembly of Michael."[54] In the position where this phrase would occur, the Bible has "to the assembly of the firstborn who are enrolled in heaven, and to God the judge of all." Both this passage and the "enduring substance" passage involve information about the heavenly worlds.

I call these misattributions because of the virtually unanimous opinion among biblical scholars that Paul did not write Hebrews. Hebrews has a much more ornate literary style than Paul's letters, and is differently paced and argued, than the writings widely acknowledged to be Paul's.[55] Some scholars currently debate whether Paul wrote Colossians or Ephesians[56] or even the Pastoral Epistles,[57] but no one (to my knowledge) still supports Pauline authorship of Hebrews. The early church did not hold to it, but in the fourth century some church fathers attributed it to Paul, probably because of Hebrews's heavy use of the sacrificial metaphor, and that attribution became the standard view. Some *UB* authors in Part 3 are utilizing the ecclesiastical tradition rather than scholarship, in attributing Hebrews to Paul.

One proposed solution to this problem (which I consider unlikely) is that the author of Hebrews incorporated some fragments from a writing of Paul's, and that the particular passages quoted in the *UB* were indeed Paul's. I think it more likely that the *UB* authors needed to make certain points from the Bible, and just followed church tradition in attributing the authorship to Paul. They were not concerned with precise and total historical accuracy, but with communicating essential

---

[54] *UB* 47:10.3 (539:5). The author is "a Brilliant Evening Star."

[55] Hebrews is generally treated as a sermon, rather than a letter, with an anonymous author. Scholars used to refer to the seven "undisputed letters" (Romans, 1 Corinthians, 2 Corinthians, Galatians, Philippians, 1 Thessalonians, and Philemon), but this term may be passing out of usage, since there seems to be less consensus about authorship than there was thirty years ago. Some scholars are arguing for co-authorship for some letters, such as Colossians. There is also the very complex matter of the later redaction (editing and amending) of the letters.

[56] Manovandet Melchizedek attributes an Ephesians passage ("spiritual hosts of wickedness in the heavenly places" [Eph 6:12] to Paul (*UB* 53:9.2 [611:1]). I would guess that only about 30% of NT scholars consider Paul the author of Ephesians.

[57] A minority of scholars, perhaps 20%, still support Pauline authorship of the Timothy and Titus letters. *UB* 130:5.1 (1436:2) speaks of "the harsh words which Paul later spoke," referring to Titus 1:12.

meanings. They refer to "Paul" in those cases where church traditions attributed the writings to Paul. Thus, when the *UB* says "Paul," it really refers to the Pauline *tradition*, whoever the actual author might be. The motives of the *UB* authors are religiously instructional rather than fastidiously factual, especially when it concerns a detail that they do not consider of great importance. But the actual authorship of particular passages *is* important to scholarship.

And actual Pauline authorship is also important to a Melchizedek, the only author in Part III who separates Hebrews from Paul: "But one of the writers of the Book of Hebrews understood the mission of Melchizedek."[58] He does not attribute Hebrews to Paul, and he clearly indicates that there is more than one author for Hebrews.

On the non-Pauline authorship of Hebrews the midwayers are in agreement with the Melchizedek. In speaking about the predominantly Pauline character of the New Testament, they list "the Book of Hebrews" as one of the exceptions.[59] It is fair to say that the primary *UB* experts on strictly *biblical* subject matter are the midwayers and Melchizedeks, and that they know the subject matter better than do the authors of the papers on the anthropology of religion (a Brilliant Evening Star, an Archangel, and a Life Carrier).

While the authorship of Hebrews is not central to the theme of this paper, this information sheds light on the way the various *UB* authors utilized human sources. It shows that the idiosyncrasies of the human sources were sometimes carried over into the *UB* text, although the bulk of our study will show many more instances where idiosyncrasies were *not* carried over.

2. Late Nineteenth and Early Twentieth Century Scholarship on Paul

2.1 Renan: the historical Jesus and Paul

The popular nineteenth century writer Ernest Renan raised many of the questions that later writers pursued. Renan was an important

---

[58] *UB* 93:9.11 (1024:2).

[59] *UB* 196:2.1 (2091:10).

initiator of the modern re-examination of Jesus and Paul, freed from the constructs of schools of theology, whether orthodox or liberal. Renan was largely negative about all the developed theology of Christianity, though he approved of the supposedly simple serenity and spirituality of Jesus.

Renan is a rationalist and a skeptic, though he coats it with sentimental and poetic observations. He is hostile to national peculiarities, whether Greek or Jewish. This reflects a view that is common among believers and liberal scholars. It states that, in order to be a universalistic religion available to all nationalities, Christianity developed a method for de-nationalizing the useful ideas of its constituent groups and drawing them into the orthodox orbit. Christianity is largely the story of the universalizing of certain key Jewish religious beliefs as well as Greek philosophic ideas, Roman ethics and administrative methods, and mystical sacramental intuitions. This was indeed a common technique of Christian assimilation of existing ideas, and remains an unconscious mental pattern even among those (like Renan) who have left Christian doctrine behind.

Renan represents a type that is frequently encountered in Christendom: intellectually enlightened but somewhat unaware of his own prejudices, including an anti-Jewish bias. He overstates the facts when he says that, for Paul, "Christ, by killing the law, therefore freed us from the law."[60] It is true that Paul recognized Torah-observance as an ethnic barrier between Jews and Gentiles, a barrier made obsolete by the new salvation in Christ. Nevertheless, Paul saw Christ as the fulfillment of Jewish law and prophecy, and all his explanations of the changed religious situation were argued on a basis in Jewish scripture.

Renan said that the summary of true Christianity was not the Epistle to the Romans but the Sermon on the Mount. While the *UB* authors would share the sentiment, they may be countering an over-attention to the Sermon when they write that, "The so-called 'Sermon

---

[60] Ernest Renan, *Origins of Christianity, volume III: Saint Paul* (NY: Carleton, Publ., 1869), 276.

on the Mount' is not the gospel of Jesus. . . . It was Jesus' ordination charge to the twelve apostles."[61]

At the end of his book on Paul, Renan wrote that the age of Paul was coming to an end, and that what was permanent in Christianity would outlive Paul's influence. He concludes "the writings of Paul have been . . . the cause of the principal defects of Christian theology."[62] These statements of Renan's provoked much reflection and response among lay readers as well as scholars.

Finally, Renan drew attention to the early rivalry between Christianity and one of the mystery cults: Mithraism, pointing out that "its resemblances with Christianity are so striking, that Saints Justin and Tertullian call it a satanic plagiarism. Mithraism had its baptism, its Eucharist, its *agape*, its penitence, its expiations, its unctions."[63] But he points to Greek paganism when he says "the layer of Christianity which covers the old Pagan basis is here very superficial."[64]

Renan's was just one of a number of voices that rose up in the late 19th century and expressed strong criticism of the Apostle Paul. Paul Lagarde in Germany made the same points but even more forcefully and with an anti-Semitic edge. And Nietzsche initiated another type of hostility to Paul, "the first Christian. . . a mind as superstitious as it was cunning. . . [for whom] the intractable lust for power reveals itself as an anticipatory revelling in *divine* glories."[65]

Further discussion of Nietzsche would take us away from our central concern. It is important to note, however, that, by the turn of the century, negative criticism of Paul was not unusual.

---

[61] *UB* 140: 4.1 (1572:1).

[62] Renan, *Origins, Saint Paul, vol. 3,* 330.

[63] My translation of Ernest Renan, *Marc-Aurèle et La Fin Du Monde Antique* (Paris: Calmann Lévy, 1891), 576–77.

[64] Renan, *Origins, Saint Paul, vol. 3,* 144.

[65] Friedrich Nietzsche, *Daybreak: Thoughts on the Prejudices of Morality* (Cambridge: Cambridge University, 1982), 39, 41–42.

2.2 The History of Religions School: the Skepticism of Wrede

The most important stream of biblical scholarship emanating from the nineteenth century was the History of Religions school. It was of German origin but gained many British and American adherents. The essential point of this school was that religions borrow from each other, and the study of any religion can be illuminated by studying the whole religious milieu in a region. Similarity of concepts and expressions among religions usually meant a borrowing in one or both directions.

G. Anrich raised questions of mystery religion influence with his *Das antike Mysterienwesen in seinem Einfluss auf das Christentum* in 1894. Albrecht Dieterich said Paul's "elemental spirits" (Gal 4:9) can only be understood against the background of contemporary views about magic and the stars as demonic powers.[66]

Paul Wendland insisted "that oriental gnosis had its influence on the special religiosity of Paul and that this factor helps to explain the undeniable difference between Paul's Christianity and Jesus' Gospel"; Christian redemption theology must be seen against a background of "purely pagan mysticism."[67]

William Wrede did not say those things, but he was a major representative of this field, and must be examined. Wrede affirmed a radical break between Jesus and Paul. He made an impression with his book on Paul, titled *Paulus* in German or simply *Paul* in English[68]. He was arguing against the liberal viewpoint, as represented by the great scholar Adolf von Harnack. Harnack saw the central teaching of Jesus as consisting in the Fatherhood of God and the infinite value of the individual, an idea that is affirmed in the *UB*'s description of "the cardinal features of the gospel. . . The pre-eminence of the individual [and] spiritual fellowship with God the Father."[69] The *UB* accepts

---

[66] Cited in Werner Georg Kümmel, *The New Testament: the History of the Investigation of Its Problems* (Nashville: Abingdon, 1972), 246.

[67] This translation by Kümmel, *The New Testament*, 247, from an 1895 work of Wendland.

[68] William Wrede, *Paul* (London: Philip Green, 1907).

[69] *The Urantia Book* 170:4.6–9 (1863:6–9); and Jesus "aimed at the emergence of the individual" 195:1.1 (2071:1).

many of the central points of liberal scholars like Harnack. The perception of the essence of the gospel as being the Fatherhood of God and Brotherhood of Man is a central tenet of liberal theology of the 1890s to 1930s. Liberal scholarship tended to see Paul as the "expounder and successor of Jesus," but Wrede rejects that view, emphasizing discontinuity over continuity.[70]

One commentator says Harnack saw "Paul's theology as the apriori legitimate continuation and interpretation of the proclamation of Jesus. Whenever the 'liberals' did perceive a difference between Jesus and Paul, it was a difference in form only."[71] But Wrede saw Paul as "the second founder of Christianity."[72] "We need not repeat that the life-work and life-picture of Jesus did *not* determine the Pauline theology."[73] Jesus' gospel was moral, Paul's was cosmic and redemptive. Paul thought he was "the proclaimer and interpreter" of Jesus, but he was in fact "the essentially new beginning."[74]

Wrede does not speak of Paul utilizing mystery cult imagery, but he accepts that some of his converts might have seen "the Lord's Supper as a pendant to the numerous solemn meals of the cults."[75] It was as a historian, not as an enemy of Paul, that Wrede saw a fundamental discontinuity between Jesus and Paul. This perception of discontinuity persists in NT scholarship to this day, although many scholars argue against it (such as N. T. Wright).

Wrede, however, exaggerated the contrast. He argued that Jesus was a rural prophet, Paul a well-educated cosmopolitan. Thus he assigns all Christology to Paul. "In Paul the origin and nature of Christ has become celestial."[76] This divide proves to be too simplistic, and has

---

[70] Wrede, *Paul*, 157.

[71] Hans Rollmann, "*Paulus alienus:* William Wrede on Comparing Jesus and Paul," in *From Jesus to Paul: Studies in Honour of Francis Wright Beare*, eds. Peter Richardson and John C. Hurd (Waterloo, Ontario: Wilfrid Laurier University, 1984), 44.

[72] Wrede, *Paul*, 179. He goes on to say, "He has thrust that greater person, whom he meant only to serve, utterly into the background" (p. 180).

[73] Wrede, *Paul*, 165-66.

[74] A 1905 letter by Wrede to Harnack, quoted by Rollmann, "*Paulus alienus*," 44.

[75] Wrede, *Paul*, 54.

[76] Wrede, *Paul*, 168.

been justly criticized by many subsequent scholars.[77] Wrede felt the salvation myth of Christianity and its supernatural worldview "was incapable of being retained by modern men and women."[78]

The *UB* does not support these anti-supernaturalist assumptions. It also does not support Wrede's hyper-skepticism about the historicity of the Gospels, which Wrede lays out in his book on Mark.[79]

2.3 Pfleiderer and Heitmüller: Mystery Cult Influences

The specific charge of mystery cult influence on the apostle Paul received detailed attention from a German scholar, Otto Pfleiderer. He discussed the sacramentalism and the redemption ideas of the mystery cults, and their purported effects on Paul. Here I give the English titles of his three principle books that touch on this subject; the German (and then the English) dates of publication follow: *Primitive Christianity: Its Writings and Teachings in their Historical Connections*, 5 volumes, 1902 (1906-11); *The Early Christian Conception of Christ: Its Significance and Value in the History of Religion*, 1903 (1905); *Christian Origins*, 1905 (1906).

The relevant volume of *Primitive Christianity* is the second edition of the first volume, which makes bolder assertions than the first edition. The second edition was published in English in four volumes from 1906 to 1911 and was widely read by American and British scholars.

Thus, these three books arguing that Paul was influenced by the mystery religions all appeared in English in the years 1905 and 1906. This is fairly early, as regards potential human sources. Researcher Matthew Block has demonstrated that almost all of the human sources used by the *UB* authors were books (usually popular ones) published in the teens, 20s, and 30s in English. *Primitive Christianity*, however, definitely influenced some authors of the 20s and 30s on this subject. Pfleiderer anticipates many of the points made by later writers:

---

[77] See Ben Witherington III, *The Christology of Jesus* (Minneapolis: Fortress Press, 1990).

[78] Rollmann, "*Paulus alienus*," 30.

[79] William Wrede, *The Messianic Secret*. London: James Clarke, 1971.

The mystery cults . . . could be studied at that time scarcely anywhere better than in Tarsus, where Paul had lived as a youth. . . . [P]ictures of . . . heathen cults . . . impressed themselves upon his memory.[80]

In this doctrine of vicarious expiation . . . the Judaism of that period was in the closest touch with those conceptions of the contemporary paganism which underlay, especially, the expiatory ritual of the mystery cults.[81]

The Lord's Supper is a "communion of the body and blood of Christ," whereby partakers entered into a mystical union with their Head. . . The affinity of these conceptions with those of the heathen Mystery cults is obvious.[82]

Paul created a new religious world outlook whose organizing principle consists in the Christian faith in the crucified and exalted Jesus Christ, but whose elements are taken on the one hand from Pharisaic theology and on the other from Hellenistic theosophy.[83]

The following quote is given to show Pfleiderer's penetrating insight, not because there is any *UB* parallel:

From the consciousness of Paul, in which the filial Spirit of Jesus had to struggle with the legal spirit of the Pharisee, there could only spring a theory of redemption which vacillated between the two . . . fighting the legal religion with its own forms in order to open up the way for the freedom of the children of God.[84]

---

[80] Otto Pfleiderer, *Primitive Christianity: Its Writings and Teachings in their Historical Connections*, vol. 1 (NY: G. P. Putnam's Sons, 1906), 61–62. Cf. *UB* 98:7.7, 9 (1084:5, 7); 121:5.13 (1337:9).

[81] Pfleiderer, *Primitive Christianity*, 74.

[82] Pfleiderer, *Primitive Christianity*, 103. Cf. the excerpt in Kümmel, *The New Testament*, 209 bottom.

[83] Translated by Kümmel, *The New Testament*, 208, taken from *Primitive Christianity*.

[84] Pfleiderer, *Primitive Christianity*, 337.

Simultaneously, W. Heitmüller was focusing more particularly on the idea that mystery cult influence lies behind Paul's sacramentalism, causing a minor stir with his frank statements:

> The world that he had to win could not yet endure the purely spiritual view of the Gospel that corresponded most closely to his religious genius; it needed the excitement and the magic of the mysteries and sacraments. . . . The Pauline idea of the Eucharist . . . is a new sprout on an old branch of the history-of-religions tree of mankind. . . . Nascent Christianity lived in an atmosphere which . . . was impregnated with the bacilli of the mysteries.[85]

> The whole frame of mind which dominates the preaching of Jesus is of a completely different order than that of the sacramental religion. . . Jesus' circle of Judaism was free of sacramental representation.[86]

The Pauline version of the Eucharist and baptism arises from "a mystical-natural conception" and a "primitive, animistic, spiritistic way of thinking."[87] Heitmüller's remains one of the underlying source-books for assertions of mystery cult influence.

More recent scholarship also notices similarities between the Mithraic ritual and the Eucharist. "The Roman Mithraic reliefs depict the divine sacrifice which gives life to men. . . It may be that the sacrifice was thought of as a timeless act. . . that the sacrifice was viewed eschatologically."[88] "The reality for the believer was salvation

---

[85] This translation is by Kümmel, *The New Testament*, 257. The original source is W. Heitmüller, *Taufe und Abendmahl bei Paulus: Darstellung und religionsgeschichtliche Beleuchtung* (Göttingen: Vandenhoeck & Ruprecht, 1903), 36–37, 51–52.

[86] My translation of Heitmüller, *Taufe und Abendmahl*, 38–40.

[87] Translation by Kümmel, *The New Testament*, 256, from *Taufe und Abendmahl*, on or near page 36.

[88] John R. Hinnells, "Reflections on the bull-slaying scene," in *Mithraic Studies, vol. 2*, ed. John R. Hinnells (Rowman and Littlefield: Manchester University Press, 1975), 309–10.

through the ritual identification in the cult meal with the god's saving sacrifice of the eternal blood—eternal blood, for it gave eternal life."[89]

2.4 Frazer: the Myth of Resurrection

A History of Religions scholar who had a far-reaching effect was Sir James Frazer. His field was anthropology of religion, not biblical studies, but he greatly influenced NT scholarship. In a nutshell, his theory was that the "dying and rising gods" of the Middle East were conceptualizations of "the growth and decay of vegetation . . . as effects of the waxing and waning strength of divine beings."[90] There were many similarities among these gods. He briefly notes some similarities between Mithraism and Christianity, and then calls them both the "sincere, if crude, attempts to fathom the secret of the universe."[91] This is his characterization of all religion: superstition that emerged before science was available. All religion is a pseudo-science, for Frazer.

Although rarely discussing Christianity directly, his message had destructive implications for Christian orthodoxy, and this was recognized by his readers, many of whom enthusiastically accepted his books as a tool for liberation from "superstition." His assertion that the mytheme of a dying-and-rising god was widespread in the Middle East was taken up by NT scholars, and is still a hotly debated subject today. Suffice it to say that 20th century scholars have shown that Frazer exaggerated the evidence. One can no longer simply assert, without proof, that a dying-and-rising-god myth was widespread. But the Frazerian thesis, in various modified forms, was influential in the early decades of this century.

2.5 Bousset: Gentile Worship

With Bousset we have a major History of Religions scholar, who built upon previous scholars and added new ideas. He argues that the very

---

[89] Hinnells, "Reflections on the bull-slaying," 311.

[90] James G. Frazer, *Adonis, Attis, Osiris: Studies in the History of Oriental Religion* (London: Macmillan, 1906), 3.

[91] James G. Frazer, *The Golden Bough: A Study in Magic and Religion*. 1 Volume Abridged edition (NY: Macmillan, 1934), 358.

term "Lord" ("*Kyrios*") was a common title for pagan gods in the Hellenistic communities.[92]

Bousset sees most of the gospel stories as fabrications of the church. The *UB* does not support the majority of William Bousset's conclusions, yet it stands remarkably close to some of Bousset's ideas about Paul.

> The gospel of Jesus presents the (ethical) religion of the forgiveness of sins, while first in Paul Christianity is reconstructed into a "redemption" religion in the supernatural sense.[93]

> In this entire earthly manner of existence of Jesus, it is only the death that actually interests [Paul]. . . The Father in heaven whom Jesus proclaimed becomes the Father of our Lord Jesus Christ.[94]

> It is the language of the mysteries which is developed in the expressions about the Lamb of God, the blood of Christ and the cross. . . [W]idespread . . . was the idea of the necessity of atonement through a blood sacrifice.[95]

Bousset asserted that there was a widespread "Primal Man" myth,[96] upon which Paul supposedly draws, but this has no support from the *UB*. And, while the *UB* mentions some similarities between Mithras and the Christ of the NT, they nowhere support the following "Frazerian" notion:

> The myth of the suffering, dying, and rising god was extraordinarily widely distributed in the Hellenistic religious life . . . Adonis . . . Attis . . . Osiris . . . Heracles Sandan of Tarsus.[97]

---

[92] Wilhelm Bousset, *Kyrios Christos* (Nashville: Abingdon, 1970; originally published 1913), 139–50 and elsewhere.

[93] *Kyrios Christos*, 182.

[94] *Kyrios Christos*, 208–09.

[95] *Kyrios Christos*, 308–09.

[96] *Kyrios Christos*, 178, 190, 195–97 and elsewhere.

[97] *Kyrios Christos*, 188.

. . . The one idea which seizes Hellenistic superstitious piety with mystical power, the idea of the dying and rising, salvation-bringing deity.[98]

Paul Wernle is another important name in biblical studies. As regards the mystery cults, he mainly takes notice of their influence in the immediately post-Pauline period. "We have traced the first steps of that fateful development which, under the influence of Greek and Oriental mysteries, made of Christianity a religion of superstition and magic charms."[99] But he also admits that Paul opened the gate for this process when he allowed "sacred rites" to have saving power, and "Christianity in its infancy was drawn into the chaos of Oriental religions," although it was "balanced by the preponderant ethical note in the apostle's teaching and character."[100]

Wernle accuses Bousset of defining Paul's religiosity solely in terms of "History of Religions factors," and not looking seriously at "the rabbinical roots of Pauline thought, nor Paul's familiarity with a definite Christology of the primitive church."[101] But he does admit that Paul shaped Christianity as we know it, that "he first introduced Christianity into world history. . . He was the great mediator of the Gospel and, as such, gained it its place."[102]

2.6 Reitzenstein: Syncretistic Christianity

The first edition of Richard Reitzenstein's *Hellenistic Mystery-Religions* preceded Bousset's book, but the second edition is the more important and complete work, and it responds to Bousset at points. Reitzenstein's book was even bolder than Bousset's in insisting that Christianity borrowed heavily from syncretized oriental mythologies, saying that even

---

[98] *Kyrios Christos*, 189.

[99] Paul Wernle, *The Beginnings of Christianity, vol. II: The Development of the Church* (New York: G. P. Putnam's Sons, 1904), 132.

[100] Wernle, *The Beginnings of Christianity, vol. II*, 128.

[101] Quoted in Kümmel, The New Testament, 316. The original source is "Jesus und Paulus," ZThK 25 (1919), 90.

[102] My translation of Wernle's, *Die Anfänge unserer Religion* (Tübingen und Leipzig: J. C. B. Mohr [Paul Siebeck], 1904), 256.

its concept of redemption is borrowed from Gnosticism. He asserted, "Since the appearance of Dieterich's classic book, *Eine Mithrasliturgie*, there is hardly any need for new proof that Paul was familiar with the language of the mystery religions and constantly made use of this acquaintance."[103] Once one accepts that "Christianity in its origins is an Oriental religion,"[104] the finding of numerous similarities with other religions is not surprising. He argued that the individualism, universalism, and mysticism common in Hellenistic religion also occur in the religious viewpoint of Greek Christians, and "Persian dualism and Babylonian belief in the stars play a crucial role."[105]

As regards Paul, Reitzenstein notices a definite commingling of Jewish, Greek, and Oriental elements.

> In the work of Paul himself we may trace out the relationship to the mystery religions, not in the sacraments in themselves, but only in the figurative language and in individual, unique words. . . "putting on" . . . the heavenly body which was cultically represented in the mystery religions . . . "the body of death", which is found also among Mandaeans and Manichaeans.[106]

He finds that Paul's dual-consciousness, as when he contrasts his own weakness with the power of God in him, is similar to what is found in "the mystery-religions, and we find it also in the gnosticism that grew out of them."[107] His references to Paul's supposed affinities with Gnosticism, and especially with Mandaeanism, were attacked by other scholars on the grounds of anachronism. Reitzenstein is using 2nd to 4th century Gnostic evidence and 4th century and later Mandaean evidence to draw parallels to the first century apostle. This is a valid criticism, and it weakens Reitzenstein's case, but does not destroy it. Paul's

---

[103] Richard Reitzenstein, *Hellenistic Mystery-Religions: their basic ideas and significance*. Based on the Second German Edition. (Pittsburgh: The Pickwick Press, 1978), 79.

[104] Reitzenstein, *Hellenistic Mystery-Religions*, ix.

[105] Reitzenstein, *Hellenistic Mystery-Religions*, 67.

[106] Reitzenstein, *Hellenistic Mystery-Religions*, 78–79.

[107] Reitzenstein, *Hellenistic Mystery-Religions*, 83.

use of mystery terminology (which can be so designated on the strength of first and second century evidence) still needs to be explained.

> As is known, in II Cor. 3:18 Paul describes that material transformation which must already here on earth have occurred with the Christian. . . . The expression metamorfoúmeqa . . . is common in the language of the mysteries.[108]

It is not any one such observation, but the sum total of such observations by Reitzenstein, that gives support to his argument that Paul utilizes oriental-Gentile thought patterns, though subjecting them to the alchemy of his Jewish-Christian beliefs.

The *UB* never supports the assertion of Pauline borrowing from Mandaean religion, nor Reitzenstein's belief that a particular Persian legend lies behind the redeemer story, and it does not refer to "gnosticism" (by that name) at all, but it does support the notion that mystery-religion influenced Paul, and thus Christianity.

19th-century German scholarship led the way in describing the religious milieu of Paul's time, but with the 20th century, great scholars in France, Britain and the U.S. made major contributions. The Belgian Franz Cumont wrote many books on Greco-Roman religion and an important one on Mithraism. He emphasized the role of Mithraism and other mysteries in the Roman empire, rather than any similarities to Christianity, but his work had implications in that direction, and others utilized his work to draw attention to similarities.

2.7 Successors and Critics of Reitzenstein

A number of authors wrote popularizing restatements of the work of Bousset, Cumont, and Reitzenstein in the 1920s, including Arthur Weigall (*The Paganism in Our Christianity*)[109] and Thomas Wilson (*St. Paul and Paganism*).[110] In France, Alfred Loisy wrote about pagan mys-

---

[108] Reitzenstein, *Hellenistic Mystery-Religions*, 454.

[109] Arthur Weigall, *The Paganism in our Christianity* (New York: G. P. Putnam's Sons, 1928).

[110] Thomas Wilson, *St. Paul and Paganism* (Edinburgh: T & T Clark, 1927).

teries and Christian mysteries, arguing for the influence of Orphism upon the Christian Eucharist. On the subject of the Eucharist, he became the principal articulator of a theory of mystery cult influence, and of the biblical texts having been altered in a liturgical direction.[111] L. Patterson protested that "St. Paul would be irreconcilably opposed to any heathen rites."[112] This is true, but does not negate the possibility of borrowing without crediting the source. H. Kennedy wrote a book debunking most of the conclusions of Reitzenstein,[113] while A. Nock argued for Paul's "unfamiliarity with the mysteries."[114]

Many scholars accepted only a portion of Reitzenstein's ideas. Nor did everyone perceive a literary parallel where Reitzenstein perceived one. Most scholars felt Reitzenstein's thesis that Christianity had taken on "the redeemed redeemer" of early Gnosticism was not sufficiently proven by Reitzenstein.

Hastings Rashdall in England wrote a study of atonement theories (*The Idea of Atonement*); at the end of his book he allowed that Paul borrowed mystery terminology, but not that his thought was influenced in any essential way by mystery cults.[115]

Kirsopp Lake focused on the Gentile reception of Christianity. He insisted, "many of the Greeks must have regarded Christianity as a superior form of 'Mystery Religion'"; the Gentile would have seen "every reason for equating the Lord with the Redeemer-God of the Mystery Religions."[116] In Christianity, "Hellenism . . . lives on; for it was the genius of Christianity to weld together . . . Stoic ethics . . .

---

[111] Alfred Loisy, *The Birth of the Christian Religion* (London: Allen & Unwin, 1948), 224, 247–50.

[112] L. Patterson, *Mithraism and Christianity: A Study in Comparative Religion* (Cambridge: Cambridge University Press, 1921), 54.

[113] H. A. A. Kennedy, *St. Paul and the Mystery Religions* (London: Hodder & Stoughton, 1913).

[114] Arthur Darby Nock, "Early Gentile Christianity and its Hellenistic Background," in *Essays on Religion and the Ancient World I* (Cambridge: Harvard University Press, 1972), 101.

[115] Hastings Rashdall, *The Idea of the Atonement in Christian Theology* (London: Macmillan, 1919), 481–84, 488–91.

[116] Kirsopp Lake, *The Earlier Epistles of St. Paul: their motive and origin.* 2nd edition (London: Rivingtons, 1919), 45, 44.

Platonic metaphysics . . . Oriental mysticism . . . the faith and hope of Israel."[117]

In Germany, Rudolf Bultmann actually used the presence or absence of mystery elements as a way of distinguishing Jesus from Paul: "what distinguishes it [Jesus' religion] from Paul, distinguishes it also in part from the Mysteries."[118] Even though Bultmann is most well-known for his skepticism about the historical value of the Gospels, he did describe Jesus as a Jewish prophet, with a strong emphasis on eschatology but not manifesting the interest in fantastic details of the afterlife such as one finds in apocalyptic literature. He never changed his view that the Pauline communion sacrament stood under a mystery influence:

[I]n the mysteries it . . . is communion with a once dead and risen deity, in whose fate the partaker receives a share through the sacramental meal. . . Paul himself shows that the sacrament of the Lord's Supper stands in this context . . . not only by calling the Lord's Supper "the table of the Lord," thereby using a Hellenistic term for cultic banquets (1 Cor 10:21 . . .), but especially by the way he contrasts the cup and table of the Lord with heathen sacrificial meals . . . these make the partakers "partners (or communicants) with demons."[119]

The facts and teachings of Jesus' life were unimportant, for Paul; only the death and Resurrection mattered, in forming the content of "our mystery" (1 Cor 2:7). "The incarnation is never accorded a meaning independent of the crucifixion. . . All that is important for him in the story of Jesus is the fact that Jesus was born a Jew and lived under the Law (Gal 4:4) and that he had been crucified (Gal 3:1; 1 Cor 2:2)."[120]

---

[117] F. J. Foakes-Jackson and Kirsopp Lake, *The Beginnings of Christianity: Part I: The Acts of the Apostles*. Vol. I: *Prolegomena I: The Jewish, Gentile and Christian Backgrounds* (London: Macmillan, 1920), 262.

[118] Quoted in Kümmel, *The New Testament*, 352. The original source is *Exegetics*.

[119] Rudolf Bultmann, *Theology of the New Testament*, vol. 1 (NY: Charles Scribner's Sons, 1951), 148.

[120] Bultmann, *Theology 1*, 293, 188.

2.8 Measured Responses by Peabody and Inge

The Harvard professor Francis Peabody picked up not only the History of Religions teaching, but also some Frazerian ideas. He speaks of Paul's "brilliant adaptations from Oriental mythology."[121] As do many other authors, he says "the elaborate rites and mythologies of these redemptive dramas must have been familiar in Paul's city of Tarsus."[122] Still, Peabody has a great respect for Paul's religious instincts: "he utilizes the language and accepts the forms of the mystery-religions . . . but at once proceeds to enrich them with a moral quality of which Oriental religion gives no sign."[123] Speaking of the later church, he bemoans "the persistent inclination to identify religion with mystery and miracle and to make it an instrument of sacerdotal authority."[124] Sometimes the critique of these Protestant scholars reflects their debate with Catholicism, the sacerdotal religion *par excellence*. I will say more about this in the section on J. Z. Smith.

The British cleric William Inge accepts some of the conclusions of the History of Religions School.

> It is useless to deny that St. Paul regarded Christianity as, at least on one side, a mystery-religion. Why else would he have used a number of technical terms which his readers would recognise at once as belonging to the mysteries? Why else should he repeatedly use the word 'mystery' itself, applying it to doctrines distinctive of Christianity. . . ? . . . It was as a mystery-religion that Europe accepted Christianity.[125]

This last sentence, of course, does not necessarily implicate Paul, but that Inge *does* see Paul implicated is shown by the following:

---

[121] Francis Greenwood Peabody, *The Apostle Paul and the Modern World* (NY: Macmillan, 1923), 34.

[122] Peabody, *The Apostle Paul*, 31.

[123] Peabody, *The Apostle Paul*, 208.

[124] Peabody, *The Apostle Paul*, 210.

[125] William Ralph Inge, "St. Paul (1914)," in *Outspoken Essays* (volume 1) (London: Longmans, Green & Co., 1920), 227.

St. Paul, who was ready to fight to the death against the Judaising of Christianity, was willing to take the first step and a long one, towards the Paganizing of it. . . He does not appear to see any danger in allowing . . . the worship of Christ . . . to [be] set in [a mystery] framework, provided only that they have no part nor lot with those who sit at "the table of demons"—the sacramental love feasts of the heathen mysteries.[126]

Yet it was just those love-feasts which embodied the communal unity which was the principal common element between Christianity and the mysteries.[127]

The *UB* does not appear to ever quote Inge, but their conclusions are very similar. Both saw Paul as an ardent religious genius who conveyed some of the teachings of Jesus, but who took the first step toward paganizing the religion. Inge implies that the real corruption came after Paul's lifetime, but that he opened the gate to these influences: "he does not appear to have foreseen the unethical and polytheistic developments of sacramental institutionalism."[128]

Another fairly balanced approach is that of T. R. Glover, who mentions all the religious influences available at the time of Christianity's origins, including the mystery cults of Isis and Cybele.[129]

2.9 A Contemporary Corrective: J. Z. Smith

Jonathan Z. Smith is a current scholar who endeavors to show that the logic of Frazer, Pfleiderer and the rest, is deeply flawed. (His motive does not seem to be theological; Smith is not a defender of orthodoxy.) "The Protestant . . . enterprise of comparing the religions of

---

[126] Inge, "St. Paul," 228.

[127] Inge, "St. Paul," 227.

[128] Inge, "St. Paul," 228.

[129] T. R. Glover, *The Conflict of Religions in the Early Roman Empire* (London: Methuen, 1909).

Late Antiquity and early Christianities has been an affair of mythic conception and ritual practice from the outset."[130]

Frazer's assumption that there was a widespread anxiety-induced worship of the Cornspirit is doubtful. His assertion that there was a plethora of "dying-and-rising saviour gods" is more than doubtful, it is simply false, according to Smith. Even the mystery deities Mithras, Adonis, Osiris, Attis, who were assumed to be the quintessential dying-and-rising gods, turn out not to match this paradigm at all (except for Osiris). The Attis myth involves a partial mitigation, but not overcoming, of death. Attis did not rise again, but manifested limited signs of life: his hair still grew, and his little finger would move; the element of "dying and rising . . . turns out to be . . . a third or fourth century development."[131] I think the Attis question is complicated, and Smith's utter rejection of a resurrection element early in the cult's history (he is relying on a book by Gasparro in this matter) is just as peremptory as previous lumpings-together of Attis with Osiris and Adonis. Still, it is necessary that the sloppiness of Frazer's methods be exposed, and the soundness of his conclusions questioned.

Smith also lambastes the work of those more conservative scholars who argued against the mystery cult thesis. He criticizes Arthur D. Nock and Raymond Brown, who argued that Paul's use of the term "mysterion" can be completely explained on the basis of the Septuagint, and need not involve any pagan influence.[132] Nock's and Brown's arguments are hard to maintain, given that the usage they point to is primarily in *one chapter* of the Septuagint (Daniel 2).[133] Nock treats the Septuagint and NT as though they were "an enclosed world . . . a ghetto culturally and linguistically" shielded from pagan influences.[134]

---

[130] Jonathan Z. Smith, *Drudgery Divine: on a Comparison of Early Christianities and the Religions of Late Antiquity* (School of Oriental and African Studies, University of London, 1990), 143.

[131] Smith, *Drudgery Divine*, 101–03, 126–9; the quote is from 103.

[132] Nock, "Early Gentile Christianity"; Raymond Brown, *The Semitic Background of the term "Mystery" in the New Testament*. Facet Books Biblical Series 21 (Philadelphia: Fortress, 1968), especially pages 6–12, 34–37, 41–44.

[133] Smith, *Drudgery Divine*, 73-74.

[134] Smith, *Drudgery Divine*, 70-71.

Smith finds the whole argument, both on the radical side and on the conservative side, to be "an enterprise undertaken in bad faith," unworthy of the name of "scholarship."[135] I think this judgment is a bit extreme, especially as regards his utter rejection of the work of Pfleiderer, but he raises many valid questions, and his book is of great importance in this discussion.

3. Possible Human Sources Used

There is a possibility that Pfleiderer or Peabody could be among the human sources utilized in *The Urantia Book*. Even more likely are the following candidates.

3.1 Bacon: the Two Gospels

The supreme problem in the history of our religion is how it could change so profoundly in the brief space that can be allowed between the preaching of the gospel of the kingdom by Jesus in Galilee, and the gospel that Paul referred to in First Corinthians as received by him in the beginning, the redemption faith he expressly says was common to all disciples. The one is a gospel *of* Jesus, and the other a gospel *about* Jesus.[136]

This last line has become almost a slogan and has been repeated by many people,[137] although I cannot be certain that Bacon originated it. The concept is not original with him; we encountered it in Wrede, Bousset, and others. But Bacon's formulation may be the source of the *UB*'s version: "All Urantia is waiting for the proclamation of . . . not the gospel about Jesus, but the living, spiritual reality of the gospel of

---

135 Smith, *Drudgery Divine*, 143.

136 Benjamin W. Bacon, *Jesus and Paul: Lectures Given at Manchester College, Oxford, for the Winter Term, 1920* (NY: Macmillan, 1921), 33–34. Cf. the passage in Bacon's *The Making of the New Testament* (London: Williams and Norgate, 1912), 53: "the gospel *of* Jesus . . . in . . . an Aramaic compilation . . . the gospel *about* Jesus, represented in the Pauline Epistles, and these based on their author's personal experience."

137 Even Alan Watts used it, in his last article. "The Church . . . adopted a religion *about* Jesus instead of the religion *of* Jesus" (Alan Watts, "The World's Most Dangerous Book," in *Playboy* 20 [1973]: 278). Watts, however, might have known about *The Urantia Book*, and borrowed the line from there.

Jesus."[138] The other words in Bacon do not appear in the *UB*, and the *UB*'s stirring rhetoric preceding that line does not come from Bacon. That Paul's gospel of redemption by means of the atoning death of Jesus does not appear in Jesus' own teachings, is a point of agreement. But Bacon seems to accept Paul's assertion (1 Cor 15:3) that he merely inherited the idea, while Part 4 of the *UB* seems to attribute the doctrine to Paul himself. More important divergences emerge upon examination. Bacon thought Jesus' gospel was purely ethical and social, while Paul's was "a religion of personal salvation" and dealt with eternal life. The *UB* would never disassociate Jesus from personal salvation or from the teaching of eternal life.

Bacon's sources include Pfleiderer, Wrede, and Wernle.

The "of-versus-about" axiom in the *UB* could come from Bacon, in which case he would be the human source for a saying that is repeated a number of times in the *UB*.

3.2 Walter Bundy

In a book published one year later than Bacon's, Bundy makes a similar statement.

There is no doubt that the last paper of the *UB* makes extensive use of Bundy's *The Religion of Jesus*, and numerous parallel passages can be cited,[139] for instance Bundy's "Jesus' faith in God was not something that he held, but something that held him. . . that sweeps everything before it" is utilized by the *UB*: "This faith was not reverence for tradition nor a mere intellectual belief which he held as a sacred creed, but rather a sublime experience and a profound conviction which *securely held him. . .* it absolutely swept away any spiritual doubts."[140] Bundy's book was written at a time when much was being written about the teachings of Jesus, and the *UB* makes use of some of these books. Unique to Bundy, and seized upon by the authors of the final paper, was Bundy's emphasis that we need to look not only at Jesus' teachings

---

[138] *UB* 94:12.7 (1041:5).

[139] As seen on Matthew Block's Urantia Book Sources site: https://urantiabooksources.com/wp-content/uploads/2020/09/196.pdf.

[140] Walter E. Bundy, *The Religion of Jesus* (Indianapolis: The Bobbs-Merrill Co., 1928), 98; *UB* 196:0.5 (2087:5).

but at his personal religious life, his wholehearted trust in the Father. "Jesus as a religious personality was infinitely more than his religious teaching."[141]

When we turn to what Bundy says on Paul, we find many points of similarity to the *UB* angle, but we are hard pressed to find a single passage that was directly utilized, and nothing on the mysteries. We find a similarity of viewpoint, but no lexical similarity, in this passage:

> In sharpest contrast with Paul's scheme of mediatorial salvation stands Jesus' childlike picture of God as the shepherd who goes into the wilderness and seeks till he finds the lost sheep, as the father who hastens to meet the lost son and welcomes him home.[142]

However, the *UB* never paints Jesus as a country bumpkin, a sincere but simple prophet, as Bundy (following in the footsteps of Wrede) does. Bultmann perpetuates this view, and it is accepted by many of today's scholars. Other scholars, however, point out the likelihood that Jesus spoke Greek, visited the large mixed cities that were not far from Nazareth, and could hardly have been as simple as Wrede portrays him. And Bundy seems to overstate the extent of Paul's Hellenization: "Even Paul was more Greek than Jew in his conception of the person of Christ."[143]

The closest to a quoted passage on Paul that I can find is this:

> Most of our Christian theology comes from Paul, but Paul never thought that he would become Christianity's first great theologian. It never occurred to him that his formulations of his own personal faith would become normative for later Christian thought.[144]

---

[141] Bundy, *Religion of Jesus*, ix.

[142] Bundy, *Religion of Jesus*, 94.

[143] Bundy, *Religion of Jesus*, 271.

[144] Bundy, *Religion of Jesus*, 288–89.

Paul little dreamed that his well-intentioned letters to his converts would someday be regarded by still later Christians as the "word of God."[145]

But Bundy is making a different overall point than the *UB* here; he goes on to defend the personal nature of Paul's religion; his sayings about Christian participation in the crucifixion and resurrection "were actual, not theoretical."[146] The *UB* also pays attention to Paul's personal religion: "the doctrines of early Christianity were generally based on the personal religious experience of three different persons: Philo of Alexandria, Jesus of Nazareth, and Paul of Tarsus."[147]

In Bundy's other book he takes a page from Wrede in pointing out how little usage Paul makes of Jesus' teachings.

He is constantly admonishing his readers to pray, but not once does he point to Jesus' words on prayer, his practise of prayer or his prayers. Paul's *Abba*-cry in Galatians 4,6 and Romans 8,15 is the only possibility of an echo from the prayer-experience of Jesus.[148]

Bundy again borrows a page from the more well-known scholars (Wrede? Peabody?) when he writes:

It is not to the Jesus of history but to the Christ of faith that Paul turns. He shows no lively interest in what Jesus, as a human personality, said or did or was.[149]

The *UB* authors do not echo all of these judgments about Paul, though they do draw a distinction between Jesus' religious life and Paul's, and between Jesus' teachings and Paul's.

---

[145] *UB* 98:7.9 (1084:8).

[146] Bundy, *Religion of Jesus*, 289.

[147] *UB* 5:4.14 (68:2).

[148] Walter E. Bundy, *Our Recovery of Jesus* (Indianapolis: The Bobbs-Merrill Co., 1929), 25.

[149] Bundy, *Our Recovery of Jesus*, 27.

3.3 Browne and Wright

Lewis Browne wrote a popularizing book that draws upon many of
the scholars mentioned above. He talks about a period long after Paul
when he exposes the paganization of Christianity:

> Much of the old love for Isis, and especially for Cybele, the great
> Mother of the Gods, was taken over into the church and translated
> into the worship of Mary, the Mother of Christ.... The pagan gods
> and goddesses were discreetly made over into Christian saints.[150]

Browne is used as a human source, especially in Paper 98:

> Three times a day, with especial elaborateness on the Sun-day and
> the twenty-fifth of December, the Mithras priests offered services
> in the caves. . . The flesh of a sacrificial animal was eaten, and its
> blood was drunk.[151]

This is utilized by the *UB*:

> The adherents of this cult worshiped in caves and other secret
> places, chanting hymns, mumbling magic, eating the flesh of the
> sacrificial animals, and drinking the blood. Three times a day, with
> special weekly ceremonials on the day of the sun-god and with the
> most elaborate observance of all on the annual festival of Mithras,
> December twenty-fifth.[152]

The cult of Cybele, "the Great Mother of the Gods" . . . found its chief
sanctuary on the Vatican Hill— almost on the precise spot where the
basilica of St. Peters now stands.[153] This one is paraphrased by the *UB*,
regarding: ". . .the Mother of God sect, which had its headquarters,

---

[150] Lewis Browne, *This Believing World: A Simple Account of the Great Religions of Mankind* (New York: Macmillan, 1953), 294.

[151] Browne, *This Believing World*, 111.

[152] *UB* 98:5.4 (1082:5). See https://urantiabooksources.com/wp-content/up-loads/2020/08/098.pdf.

[153] Browne, *This Believing World*, 104.

in those days, on the exact site of the present church of St. Peter's in Rome."[154]

Lewis lists Frazer, Cumont, Glover, and Renan among his sources.

Another human source for the *UB*'s sections on the mystery cults (Paper 98, sections 4–6, a Melchizedek author) is Wright's *A Student's Philosophy of Religion*. The intriguing passage about "a last supper which Mithras celebrated with the sun-god before he ascended into the heavens"[155] comes from Wright: "Mithra celebrated a Last Supper with the Sun God and other companions, after which he ascended into the heavens."[156] A Melchizedek's remarks about both Christianity and Mithraism having "altars" that "depicted the sufferings of the savior," and worshippers dipping fingers into "holy water"[157] comes from Wright (page 125).

The section "The Cult of Mithras" (*UB* 98:5) uses both Browne and Wright. These two authors are important sources behind certain papers in Part 3, but they do not seem to have been utilized in Part 4. Of course, there may be instances in Part 4 of which I am unaware, but here, once again, there is a difference between Parts 3 and 4.

With the exception of the remark about Tarsus,[158] Browne's and Wright's comments have to do with Christianity, rather than with Paul *per se*.

4. Conclusions

As stated at the beginning, the *UB* makes use of the more radical side of biblical scholarship in speaking about Paul. This radical scholarship was at the *forefront* of biblical scholarship at the turn of the nineteenth to twentieth centuries. More conservative scholars tended to move the conversation in the mid-twentieth century.

The bottom line about this whole issue, for the authors of the *UB*, is that mystery cult influence was related to the formulation of the

---

[154] *UB* 98:3.5 (1080:7).

[155] *UB* 98:5.3 (1082:4)

[156] William Kelley Wright, *A Student's Philosophy of Religion* (New York: Macmillan, 1935), 125. Cumont is one of Wright's sources.

[157] *UB* 98:6.3–4 (1083:3–4).

[158] *UB* 98:7.9 (1084:8), loosely based on Browne, This Believing World, 280.

doctrine of atonement, a doctrine they repudiate. Regarding the whole idea, their viewpoint is: "Jesus swept away all of the ceremonials of sacrifice and atonement. He destroyed the basis of all this fictitious guilt and sense of isolation in the universe by declaring that man is a child of God."[159] But their main target is the doctrine, not Paul personally. In fact, as we saw in section 1.2, a Melchizedek author in Part 3 concedes to Paul a partial recognition of this fact: "even the great advocate of the atonement doctrine realized something of this truth, for he declared that 'God was in Christ reconciling the world to himself.'"[160]

The Melchizedek is affirming the saying in 2 Cor 5:19, that God was *reconciling*, not *being* reconciled. In other words, God was not *persuaded* or manipulated.

There are, then, differing attitudes toward Paul by different authors of the *UB*. A Melchizedek credits Paul with wisdom that the midwayers do not. It seems clear that the midwayers are more negative about Paul than the Melchizedek is. This may not be a scholarly dispute, but a difference of emphasis resulting from different levels of involvement. It is possible that the midwayers, who are very close to the human level, were more surprised and chagrined by the human failure to clearly retain the message of the Master than were the Melchizedeks who have worked on many mortal worlds and have seen many examples of compromise. It is also likely that the midwayers are both *allowed* to be, and are *inclined* to be, more polemical than the higher-level Melchizedeks. The midwayers are directly involved in human civilization, and are urgently committed to seeing a return to the gospel of Jesus. The Melchizedeks seem to take a more long-term view, emphasizing that progress takes time and *includes* compromise.

Bibliography

Bacon, Benjamin W. *Jesus and Paul: Lectures Given at Manchester College, Oxford, for the Winter Term, 1920*. New York: The Macmillan Company, 1921.

---

[159] *UB* 103:4.4 (1133:4).

[160] *UB* 98:7.1 (1083:6); and 2 Cor 5:19. The point is that Paul recognizes God was not persuaded in any way; God was acting upon God's own will.

_____. *The Making of the New Testament*. London: Williams and Norgate. Home University Library of Modern Knowledge, 1912.

Block, Matthew. Urantia Book Sources Website: urantiabooksources.com.

Bousset, Wilhelm. *Kyrios Christos*, tr. John E. Steely. Nashville: Abingdon Press, 1970; originally published 1913.

Browne, Lewis. *This Believing World: A Simple Account of the Great Religions of Mankind*. New York: The Macmillan Company, 1953.

Bundy, Walter E. *Our Recovery of Jesus*. Indianapolis: The Bobbs-Merrill Co., 1929.

_____. *The Religion of Jesus*. Indianapolis: The Bobbs-Merrill Co., 1928.

Edersheim, Alfred. *The Life and Times of Jesus the Messiah*, Volume One. Eighth Edition. New York: Longmans, Green and Co., 1907.

Foakes-Jackson, F. J. and Kirsopp Lake, *The Beginnings of Christianity: Part I: The Acts of the Apostles*. Five volumes. Vol. I: *Prolegomena I: The Jewish, Gentile and Christian Backgrounds*. London: Macmillan and Co, 1920.

Frazer, James G. *Adonis, Attis, Osiris: Studies in the History of Oriental Religion*. The Macmillan Company, 1906.

_____. *The Golden Bough: A Study in Magic and Religion*. One Volume Abridged edition. New York: The Macmillan Company, 1934.

Glover, T. R. *The Conflict of Religions in the Early Roman Empire*. London: Methuen, 1909.

Heitmüller, W. *Taufe und Abendmahl bei Paulus: Darstellung und religionsgeschichtliche Beleuchtung. Göttingen*: Vandenhoeck & Ruprecht, 1903.

Hinnells, John R. "Reflections on the bull-slaying scene." In *Mithraic Studies, vol. 2*, edited by John R. Hinnells, 290–312. Rowman and Littlefield: Manchester University Press, 1975.

Inge, William Ralph. "St. Paul (1914)." In *Outspoken Essays* (volume 1), 205–29. London: Longmans, Green & Co., 1920.

Kennedy, H. A. A. *St. Paul and the Mystery Religions*. London: Hodder & Stoughton, 1913.

Kümmel, Werner Georg. *The New Testament: the History of the Investigation of Its Problems*. Nashville: Abingdon Press, 1972.

Lake, Kirsopp. *The Earlier Epistles of St. Paul: their motive and origin*. Second edition. London: Rivingtons, 1919.

Loisy, Alfred. *The Birth of the Christian Religion*. London: Allen & Unwin, 1948.

Nietzsche, Friedrich. *Daybreak: Thoughts on the Prejudices of Morality*. Cambridge: Cambridge University Press, 1982.

Nock, Arthur Darby. "Early Gentile Christianity and its Hellenistic Background," in *Essays on Religion and the Ancient World I*, 49–133. Cambridge: Harvard University Press, 1972.

Patterson, L. *Mithraism and Christianity: A Study in Comparative Religion*. Cambridge: Cambridge University Press, 1921.

Peabody, Francis Greenwood. *The Apostle Paul and the Modern World*. New York: The Macmillan Company, 1923.

Pfleiderer, Otto. *Christian Origins*. New York: Huebsch, 1906.

_____. *The Early Christian Conception of Christ: Its Significance and Value in the History of Religion*. New York: G. P. Putnam's Sons, 1905.

_____. *Primitive Christianity: Its Writings and Teachings in their Historical Connections*, volume 1. New York: G. P. Putnam's Sons, 1906.

Rashdall, Hastings. *The Idea of the Atonement in Christian Theology*. London: Macmillan, 1919.

Reitzenstein, Richard. *Hellenistic Mystery-Religions: their basic ideas and significance*. (Based on the Second German Edition.) Translated by John Steely. Pittsburgh Theological Monograph Series 15. Pittsburgh: The Pickwick Press, 1978.

Renan, Ernest. *Marc-Aurèle et La Fin Du Monde Antique*. Paris: Calmann Lévy, 1891.

_____. *Saint Paul* (volume 3 of *Origins of Christianity*). New York: Carleton, Publisher, 1869.

Rollmann, Hans. "*Paulus alienus:* William Wrede on Comparing Jesus and Paul." In *From Jesus to Paul: Studies in Honour of Francis Wright Beare*, edited by Peter Richardson and John C. Hurd, 23–45. Waterloo, Ontario: Wilfrid Laurier University Press, 1984.

Smith, Jonathan Z. *Drudgery Divine: on a Comparison of Early Christianities and the Religions of Late Antiquity.* School of Oriental and African Studies, University of London, 1990.

Watts, Alan. "The World's Most Dangerous Book." *Playboy* 20 (1973): 119–22, 136, 278–80.

Weigall, Arthur, *The Paganism in our Christianity.* New York: G. P. Putnam's Sons, 1928.

Wernle, Paul. *Die Anfänge unserer Religion.* Tübingen und Leipzig: J. C. B. Mohr (Paul Siebeck), 1904.

_____. *The Beginnings of Christianity, vol. II: The Development of the Church.* New York: G. P. Putnam's Sons, 1904.

Wilson, Thomas. *St. Paul and Paganism.* Edinburgh: T & T Clark, 1927.

Wrede, William. *The Messianic Secret.* London: James Clarke, 1971 (originally 1901).

_____. *Paul,* translated by Edward Lummis. London: Philip Green, 1907.

Wright, William Kelley. *A Student's Philosophy of Religion.* New York: Macmillan, 1935.

PART IV

PHILOSOPHY AND THEOLOGY

Prologue IV: God's Eternal Purpose

Compiled by Stuart Kerr

I. UNIVERSE WAS MADE TO BE INHABITED

1. The universes were made to be inhabited.

❝ The myriads of planetary systems were all made to be eventually inhabited by many different types of intelligent creatures, beings who could know God, receive the divine affection, and love him in return. The universe of universes is the work of God. and the dwelling place of his diverse creatures. 'God created the heavens and formed the earth; he established the universe and created this world not in vain; he formed it to be inhabited.' ❞ (1:0.2) Isa 45:18

2. Finites exist because of the eternal purpose.

❝ The realms of the finite exist by virtue of the eternal purpose of God. Finite creatures, high and low, may propound theories, and have done so, as to the necessity of the finite in the cosmic economy, but in the last analysis it exists because God so willed. The universe cannot be explained, neither can a finite creature offer a rational reason for his own individual existence without appealing to the prior acts and pre-existent volition of ancestral beings, Creators or procreators. ❞ (115:1.4)

3. The eternal purpose is attainable by all.

66 There is in the mind of God a plan which embraces every crea-ture of all his vast domains, and this plan is an eternal purpose of boundless opportunity, unlimited progress, and endless life. And the infinite treasures of such a matchless career are yours for the striving!

The goal of eternity is ahead! The adventure of divinity attainment lies before you! The race for perfection is on! Whosoever will may enter, and certain victory will crown the efforts of every human being who will run the race of faith and trust, depending every step of the way on the leading of the indwelling Adjuster and on the guidance of that good spirit of the Universe Son, which so freely has been poured out upon all flesh. 99 (32:5.7)

II. INFINITE PLANS OF THE ETERNAL PURPOSE

1. Infinite plans of the eternal purpose.

66 Because the First Father is infinite in his plans and eternal in his purposes, it is inherently impossible for any finite being ever to grasp or comprehend these divine plans and purposes in their fullness. Mortal man can glimpse the Father's purposes only now and then, here and there, as they are revealed in relation to the outworking of the plan of creature ascension on its successive levels of universe progression. Though man cannot encompass the signif-icance of infinity, the infinite Father does most certainly fully com-prehend and lovingly embrace all the finity of all his children in all universes. 99 (2:1.10)

2. Vast scope of God's eternal purpose.

" The Father constantly and unfailingly meets the need of the differential of demand for himself as it changes from time to time in various sections of his master universe. The great God knows and understands himself; he is infinitely self-conscious of all his primal attributes of perfection. God is not a cosmic accident; neither is he a universe experimenter. The Universe Sovereigns may engage in adventure; the Constellation Father may experiment; the system head may practice; but the Universal Father sees the end from the beginning, and his divine plan and eternal purpose actually embrace and comprehend all the experiments and all the adventures of all his subordinates in every world, system, and constellation in every universe of his vast domains. " (2:1.4)

3. All creation is a part of the divine plan.

" There is a great and glorious purpose in the march of the universes through space. All of your mortal struggling is not in vain. We are all part of an immense plan, a gigantic enterprise, and it is the vastness of the undertaking that renders it impossible to see very much of it at any one time and during any one life. We are all a part of an eternal project which the Gods are supervising and outworking. The whole marvelous and universal mechanism moves on majestically through space to the music of the the meter of the infinite thought and the eternal purpose of the First Great Source and Center. " (32:5.1)

4. The glorious plan of the eternal purpose.

66 The eternal purpose of the eternal God is a high spiritual ideal. The events of time and the struggles of material existence are but the transient scaffolding which bridges over to the other side, to the promised land of spiritual reality and supernal existence. Of course, you mortals find it difficult to grasp the idea of an eternal purpose; you are virtually unable to comprehend the thought of eternity, something never beginning and never ending. Everything familiar to you has an end. 99 (32:5.2)

III. ALL THINGS UNFOLD ACCORDING TO THE ETERNAL PURPOSE

1. All things unfold according to the eternal purpose.

66 Within the bounds of that which is consistent with the divine nature, it is literally true that 'with God all things are possible.' The long-drawn-out evolutionary processes of peoples, planets, and universes are under the perfect control of the universe creators and administrators and unfold in accordance with the eternal purpose of the Universal Father, proceeding in harmony and order and in keeping with the all-wise plan of God. There is only one lawgiver. He upholds the worlds in space and swings the universes around the endless circle of the eternal circuit. 99 (3:2.2) Matt 19:26.

2. Differential execution of the eternal purpose.

❝ The reactions of a changeless God, in the execution of his eternal purpose, may seem to vary in accordance with the changing attitude and the shifting minds of his created intelligences; that is, they may apparently and superficially vary; but underneath the surface and beneath all outward manifestations, there is still present the changeless purpose, the everlasting plan, of the eternal God.

"Out in the universes, perfection must necessarily be a relative term, but in the central universe and especially on Paradise, perfection is undiluted; in certain phases it is even absolute. Trinity manifestations vary the exhibition of the divine perfection but do not attenuate it. ❞ (2:2.3)

IV. THE ETERNAL PURPOSE WILL TRIUMPH

1. The eternal purpose will triumph.

❝ In the affairs of men's hearts the Universal Father may not always have his way; but in the conduct and destiny of a planet the divine plan prevails; the eternal purpose of wisdom and love triumphs. ❞ (3:5.3)

2. God pursues the realization of an eternal purpose.

❝ The infinite and eternal Ruler of the universe of universes is power, form, energy, process, pattern, principle, presence and idealized reality. But he is more; he is personal; he exercises a sovereign will, experiences self-consciousness of divinity, executes the mandates of a creative mind, pursues the satisfaction of the realization of an eternal purpose, and manifests a Father's love and affection for his universe children. And all these more personal traits of the Father can be better understood by observing them as they were revealed in the bestowal life of Michael, your Creator Son, while he was incarnated on Urantia. " (3:6.7)

3. Predestination and free will.

" You are all subjects of predestination, but it is not foreordained that you must accept this divine predestination; you are at full liberty to reject any part or all of the Thought Adjusters' program. " (110:2.1)

4. Mission of adversity.

" The confusion and turmoil of Urantia do not signify that the Paradise Rulers lack either interest or ability to manage affairs differently. The Creators are possessed of full power to make Urantia a veritable paradise, but such an Eden would not contribute to the development of those strong, noble, and experienced characters which the Gods are so surely forging out on your world between the anvils of necessity and the hammers of anguish. Your anxieties and sorrows, your trials and disappointments, are just as much a part of the divine plan on your sphere as are the exquisite perfection and infinite adaptation of all things to their supreme purpose on the worlds of the central and perfect universe. " (23:2.12)

12

An Introduction to
The Urantia Book for
Conservative Christians

Rev. Dr. Meredith J. Sprunger

*This essay, written decades ago, examines the nature of divine
revelation as seen from a conservative biblical perspective,
and considers the impact of a new modern
revelation on our world today.*

Many devout conservative Christians recognize the superb quality of *The Urantia Book* but are understandably troubled by its revelatory claims. Many of them have written me to ask questions, express perplexity, seek help, or challenge statements made in the text. This paper summarizes my responses over the years to their honest questions and spiritual anxieties.

I should first point out, in all sincerity, that Christian conservatives and fundamentalists have maintained much of the vibrant spiritual emphasis of religion in America. My intent is therefore not to contend with their beliefs, but rather to set shared spiritual truths in a larger frame of reference. If seen from with this larger framework, it would be fair to say that *Urantia Book* believers and those who hold to a conservative theology subscribe to the same spiritual realities and are truly brothers and sisters in Christ.

Second, all Christians face the issue of authority and hierarchy. Protestants who accept the Bible as revelation do not do so because someone demanded obedience to this belief. They see the Bible as the word of God because they recognize its truths in their own hearts. The approach to *The Urantia Book* should be made in the same way. Before encountering it, no one should regard it as an authoritative "revelation." The only way to determine whether it is inspired by God is to read and study it. Faith and conviction must come from inner leading and not from authoritarian claims or demands.

How We Got Our Bible

When dealing with this question of revelation it is helpful to bear in mind how we got our Bible. Theological schools devote entire courses to this question and hundreds of books are available on the subject.

We know that the Old Testament evolved in at least three main stages over thousands of years of history; it was edited periodically by many scholars. The canon of the Old Testament was not finalized until around 90 A.D. at the Council of Jamnia where Hebrew scholars determined which books should be included in the "official" scriptures of Judaism. Also bear in mind that this process and the conclusions reached were much more complex than my brief description might lead you to believe.

The New Testament began to take shape in the early church as a series of papers and letters written by numerous people. These were circulated among believers, edited, combined, and edited again by many early scholars and church leaders. The names of various apostles were often attached to the better papers so that they would carry more authority for church members. From around 150 A.D. to 367 A.D. various scholars and bishops drew up their own lists of books that they thought should be canonical or officially recognized. Finally, Athanasius, the highly respected bishop of Alexandria, wrote an Easter letter to the churches of his diocese in the year 367 in which he discusses the books he considered canonical. This is the first list that includes all of the twenty-seven books of the New Testament as we now have it. His list, however, was in a different sequence than our current New Testament. At various church councils in the years that followed, Athanasius' list was widely adopted.

Athanasius' pastoral letter was written with the authority of a bishop, stating: "Let no one add to them [his list] or take away aught of them." Such authoritarian exhortations were considered necessary to protect the purity of revelatory teachings; and statements like the admonition in Rev. 22:18-19 were common. In a similar way, the reve-latory commission of *The Urantia Book* requested that the book be pub-lished under international copyright protection so that the purity of these teachings could be safeguarded. These precautions are not meant to imply that God ceases to enlarge the revelation of himself and spiri-tual truth to succeeding generations. The history of the Bible shows that God does progressively reveal larger truths to a developing world. Early religious leaders often used authoritarian warnings and admonitions in a pragmatic effort to protect the latest prophetic messages.

Once you understand how the content of the Bible was accumu-lated, edited, adopted, and officially approved, you realize that reve-lation is only validated by centuries of experience. Many people rec-ognize revelation immediately because the Indwelling Spirit of God confirms what they hear or read; nevertheless, it requires a long period of time to establish a *social* tradition of revelation such as the Bible now enjoys. The powerful legacy of this ancient tradition, along with the authority and prestige of the institutional church, results in an almost irresistible cultural conditioning that largely determines how the aver-age person thinks and acts.

Recognizing New Revelation

The Urantia Book, being very new, must first be evaluated by the spirit of God working in the mind and heart of each individual. As stated earlier, you should accept nothing in *The Urantia Book* or any other book unless it passes this inner test of truth. That said, I am confident that a thousand years hence we will have a solid social tradition wit-nessing to the revelatory quality of *The Urantia Book*.

Revelation is always the product of the action of God in the life of man. God has an infinite number of ways to do this. In Jesus of Naz-areth he used both genetic-physical and spiritual means to bring reve-lation to us in the form of a person. In the writings of St. Paul he used spiritual inspiration in the mind of Paul to bring us revelation in the form of brief letters to churches. In John's book of Revelation he used a vision presented to the mind of John to bring us revelation. In *The Urantia Book* he used a corps of high spirit personalities to bring about a revelation in the form of a book. God could use an endless number of other channels and manifestations to bring revelation to his mortal children. It is God's wisdom that determines the time, place, method, and form of revelation. We might speculate on why God uses particular channels and forms but this would only be an educated guess.

The spirit of God is always active in the world, and in this sense revelation is continuous—usually through inner guidance to individuals who share prophetic insights with their society. Periodically, genuine *epochal* revelations occur—such as the coming of Jesus. Such epoch-making revelations naturally have a much greater effect on our world than the continuous forms of evolutionary revelation given to individuals. A study of epochal revelation will show that each succeeding one enlarges and enhances earlier teachings.

Revelation always builds upon existing ideas, concepts, and forms of religious knowledge that are meaningful to those who receive it. As a culture expands over many generations, revelations will appear that offer more advanced concepts—including updates and corrections—in order to convey a new and more adaptive spiritual message. This is a never-ending process.

The New Fulfills and Enhances the Old

Just as the New Testament fulfills and upsteps the Old Testament, *The Urantia Book* confirms and enlarges the truths of the Bible. In fact, most people have a much greater appreciation of the Bible after reading *The Urantia Book*. I regard the Bible and *The Urantia Book* as companion volumes.

Not to recognize this close supportive relationship is to repeat an ancient error. Early in church history a wealthy shipowner by the name of Marcion headed a movement to eliminate the Old Testament from Christian literature. The wider church wisely rejected his views. Any reader of *The Urantia Book* who took this same attitude toward the Bible, in my judgment, would be making this same mistake. Indeed, there are many people who have not been interested in the Bible until after they have read *The Urantia Book*.

It is understandable that conservative religionists have a natural suspicion toward any claim of new revelation. It has become a rather common reaction that well-meaning conservatives wonder if *The*

Urantia Book could be a work of Satan. This is a reasonable attitude for those who do not have a scholarly background in religion and who have been taught to zealously defend the Bible. It is also interesting to recall that this was the same possibility raised in connection with the message of Jesus. Jesus' response to this accusation, I think, is as good as can be made. He replied that he should be judged by the fruits of his life and by the very logic of the charge against him: "How can Satan cast out Satan?" *The Urantia Book* should be judged in the same way. I believe you will find it supports the mission and message of Jesus and refutes the intentions and message of Satan. New revelations, including epochal revelation, will probably always meet the same suspicious reception given to the message of Jesus. The leaders of traditional religious institutions are likely to oppose it; but, in time, ordinary people will receive it gladly.

The Human and the Divine

A careful study of the life and teachings of Jesus reveals there is no substantive contradiction between the spiritual teachings of Jesus found in *The Urantia Book* and the Bible. Certain physical and cosmological facts or assumptions are corrected, but most important, Jesus' entire life and teachings are enlarged by *The Urantia Book*. And yet, the essential spiritual truths do not change.

For instance, Christian theologians generally affirm that Jesus was both a human and a divine personality. However, the majority of scholars in mainline churches have long recognized that the story of the immaculate conception and virgin birth were added by the early church to make his divine nature more believable for those times. But today this story is generally a stumbling block to belief in the authenticity of the biblical record of the divinity of Jesus.

The reason most mainline church theologians do not accept the virgin birth story is that only two of the four gospels record it and nowhere else in the New Testament is it referred to. The earliest gospel, Mark, and the latest gospel, John, do not mention it. If such an important event were true, one would expect all of the gospel writers to highlight it. Secondly, there are many instances of supernatural conception and virgin birth recorded in the annals of religious history. It was the characteristic method by which many ancient peoples designated the divine origin of their prophets and leaders. Paradoxically, the biblical account traces the lineage of Jesus back to David through the ancestry of Joseph, not Mary. Finally, modern Christian scholars reject the virgin birth story because it is observed that God usually uses the natural laws of his creation to work his purposes in the world.

The spiritual truth regarding the nature of Jesus is that he was both human and divine. This *The Urantia Book* strongly affirms. The book does not even mention the immaculate conception and virgin birth doctrines. It is assumed that the Father could incarnate his Son as a mortal on our world through the natural process of conception and birth. The ancient legend of virgin birth is quietly ignored while the essential spiritual truths regarding the nature of Jesus are substantiated and enhanced.

An Enlarged Spiritual Universe

The writers of the various books of the Bible labored under a primitive universe cosmology. They visualized a flat earth in the center of creation encompassed by the "firmament" of heaven. Their extremely limited astronomical knowledge naturally conditioned their interpretation of spiritual realities and personalities. Basic spiritual truths, therefore, had to be revealed to the biblical authors in such prescientific frames of reference.

The revelators of *The Urantia Book* present a cosmology that, while in general agreement with our present astronomical knowledge, goes far beyond our contemporary science in certain respects. They also clarify our knowledge of the Paradise Trinity, the pre-bestowal personality and universe status of Jesus, and the functional relationships of angels and spiritual beings in general. Although the Bible does not speak of the Trinity per se, Christian thinkers have developed the doctrine of the Trinity and naturally assumed, without specific Biblical confirmation, that the pre-incarnate Christ was the Second Person of the Trinity. The fact that the prologue of John speaks of him as the actual Creator of our universe was more or less regarded as a poetic "Logos" doctrine since most theologians regarded God the Father as the Creator. However, the authors of *The Urantia Book* tell us that this biblical description (also stated in Col. 1:16 and Heb. 1:2) of the pre-existent Christ is literally true. He is both the Creator and Savior of our local universe.

Each so-called Creator Son of a local universe is a unique creation of the Universal Father and the Eternal Son and is known as "the only begotten son" in his universe; all in this universe who choose to ascend to the Father go through the ministry and means established by this Creator-Savior Son. We are told that, even though Jesus is not the Second Person of the Paradise Trinity, his presence and power are exactly the same as that of the Eternal Son, the Second Person of the Trinity, if he were literally acting in the place of Christ in our universe. After Jesus' bestowal on our confused planet, the Father, as recorded in Matthew, placed "all authority in heaven and earth" in his hands, and he has promised one day to return to this world of his incarnation experience; both teachings are affirmed in the Urantia text. Here, again, we see that *The Urantia Book*, while correcting assumptions made due to the very limited ancient cosmology, confirms and reinforces the basic spiritual truths of the Bible.

Christ as Savior of Mankind

All Christians look to Jesus as the mediator between man and God and regard him as the Savior of mankind. But they differ in the theological explanation of this salvation. Theologians of mainline Christian churches see salvation as the gift of God through faith in Jesus, further emphasizing God's love for humanity and full acceptance of us as his mortal sons and daughters. The theologians of Christian fundamentalism regard salvation as the gift of God through faith in Jesus because he offered himself as a blood sacrifice demanded by God the Father as the price for forgiving the sins of mankind. This is known as the blood atonement doctrine in which Jesus is seen as the one who redeems humanity from the condemnation of a just and holy God.

The only Christian belief the authors of *The Urantia Book* vigorously criticize is this blood atonement theory. They do so because this doctrine distorts and slanders the great love the Universal Father has for his mortal sons and daughters. It is in fact completely incompatible with Jesus' teachings about the nature of God the Father. God's love is not subordinate to his righteousness or holiness. Love is the Universal Father's primary attitude toward all persons. Jesus is, indeed, the Savior of mankind but not a redeemer in this sense.

The blood atonement theory has its origin in the conceptual language and life experience of Paul. Coming out of the Jewish tradition and often writing with Jewish people in mind, Paul used the symbolic idea of Jesus as the "final sacrifice" in their sacrificial system as a missionary approach that made sense to those with a Jewish background. New Testament scholars today recognize that Paul did not hold a God-concept that would be compatible with a literal blood atonement doctrine. He used this sacrificial language because it was the only frame of reference acceptable to the Jews of his day. It represents his evangelical effort to relate to the thought patterns of the Jews.

As stated, most ministers in mainline Christian churches have long since abandoned this retributive concept of God. The Bible commentary most widely used in America today is *The Interpreter's Bible* published by Abingdon Press. In volume VIII, p. 510-11, the commentary on John 3:16 says, "Some of the past explanations of the gospel are not overhelpful to us now. Most of us are not at home in the Jewish sacrificial system; and metaphors drawn from it can be confusing rather than illuminating. And some of the interpretations, popular in the Middle Ages, are to us incredible, and even monstrous. So do many, with the Gospels in their hands, appear to see in them a lesser God giving himself to save us from the implacable fury and resentment of the great God, slow and hard to be appeased, and demanding his pound of flesh from someone. That is hideous heresy; and the blasphemy of blasphemies. It was in the eternal plan of God the Father that Jesus Christ lived out this purpose: 'God was in Christ, reconciling the world unto himself' (II Cor. 5:19); he was not standing sullenly aside and needing himself to be reconciled."

We should recognize that most of those who still accept a literal blood atonement theory in our day probably do so out of misunderstanding and with no intent to deny the loving nature of God. Even so, to believe that God the Father cannot or will not love man until his innocent son is brutally executed is a cruel distortion of the loving nature of the heavenly Father that Jesus revealed. By contrast, *The Urantia Book* does affirm the positive spiritual values associated with the crucifixion and man's salvation that are important to fundamentalists as well as all other Christians.

It was the Father's will that Jesus allow the Jewish leaders to dispose of him as they desired. God does not arbitrarily interfere with the premeditated intentions of man. Jesus' death on the cross demonstrates the profound love he and the Father have for man even when they were torturing and executing him. He refuses to use divine power to save himself or punish these misguided evildoers. This great love is the most powerful saving act the Father and the Son could bestow on self-willed man in this situation; it aims to eventually deliver him from his ignorance, evil, and sin and to cause man to recognize God's transcendent love and accept sonship. Salvation is something God in Christ makes possible for man. Finite man cannot save himself, but through faith he may accept this gift of eternal life. Christ is the way by which all mortals in our universe go to the Father.

On Approaching New Truth

New truth is always challenging and often threatening to traditionalists. This is both natural and good. The tried and true values of historical experience cannot and should not be easily replaced by the new and untested. But these historic truths are periodically upstepped by prophetic vision and even epochal revelation. Such growth is usually a traumatic experience for individuals, the church, and society.

Every prophet in the history of the Old and New Testaments has met with unbelief and opposition. The priests of society have regularly stoned its prophets. Then their sons of another century build monuments to honor the prophets persecuted by their forefathers. It is good to be cautious and critical; it is helpful to doubt and carefully evaluate. But we need to be open and objective enough to allow the spirit to lead us to larger truth. Jesus told his apostles that he would send the Spirit of Truth through which he would lead them to greater truths in the future. We must be sensitive to this spirit. We need to learn to recognize truth in its many forms and varying appearances.

You will find that *The Urantia Book* will stand the test of critical examination. It is rooted solidly in the traditional spiritual verities of the Christian faith that have endured for centuries. Reading and studying *The Urantia Book* will give you a deeper and larger vision of this saving faith and help you become a part of a spiritual renaissance now dawning on our world.

13

The Great Transition:
The Catholic Response to the
Urantia Revelation

Rev. James Thomas (pseudonymous)

This unique essay by an anonymous Catholic monastic and priest lays out future options for reconciling the truths of the new revelation with the worthwhile achievements of the traditional church.

This essay is offered to all of my dear *UB*-reading friends who are concerned about the relationship between the Urantia revelation and traditional Christianity, including the prospect of a transition to the full acceptance of the revelation by the church, especially the Catholic Church. Here are some ideas to consider.

The first major step in this great transition, I believe, will be the beginnings of the reception and acceptance of the *UB* as an authentic revelation. It happens that the Catholic Church, more than the Orthodox Church, is open to the phenomenon of ongoing revelation, which it recognizes in at least two types. The first is called "post-biblical" or "post-apostolic" revelation, and this can be distinguished from what the Catholic Church calls "private revelation." The many historic cases of such private revelations, especially as given to saints and prophets, refer to the *charism* of personal revelation. This special gift helps all believers live according to the church's *existing* precepts, i.e., those teachings that are sometimes known as "public revelation." The Catholic concept of private revelation overlaps somewhat with what the *UB* calls "autorevelation."[161]

---

[161] Here is one representative statement: "Truth is always a revelation: *autorevelation* when it emerges as a result of the work of the indwelling Adjuster; *epochal revelation* when it is presented by the function of some other celestial agency, group, or personality" (101:4).

What then is "public revelation"? This refers to the Word of God as found in the Bible and revealed in the sacred tradition including the ecumenical councils, and which is taught for example in our catechisms. Private revelations, on the other hand, are regarded by the church as sometimes authentic, but as I stated they can never supersede the content of public revelation. What I prefer to call "post-apostolic" revelation instead refers to *novel* truths or doctrines that are shared with us by means of grace.

To clarify how grace seems to operate in these cases, I conducted a study a few years ago on the variety of ways modern post-apostolic revelations may take place. My conclusion was that there is no one way this happens. The Holy Spirit is very creative in using different methods to communicate with us. The point here is that Catholicism has an open approach to such new revelations, both private and post-apostolic, but always moves cautiously in relation to these events. I'm sure however that the *UB* will be seen as one of these authentic revelations, though not likely anytime soon.

Second, it seems to me that according to the *UB*, not much in liturgical Christianity can be traced back to the original teachings of Jesus. In fact, what Jesus teaches in Part IV is not an ecclesiastical system at all. And yet, we have clear statements in the text that Christ "fosters" the church through the "angels of the churches" and by other means, influencing the institutions of Christianity in whatever way is helpful in each generation to facilitate our communion with the Lord and to advance his divine purposes.[162] But this relationship needs to be clarified, as I try to do below.

---

[162] These angels are also known in the *UB* as *the religious guardians*, and they are one corps among the "twelve corps of the master seraphim of planetary supervision." Taking a cue from the Bible, the text also refers to the religious guardians as "the angels of the churches" (see Rev. 1:20). The *UB* calls them "the earnest contenders for that which is and has been. They endeavor to maintain the ideals of that which has survived for the sake of the safe transit of moral values from one epoch to another. They . . . seek to translate from one generation to another the imperishable values of the old and passing forms into the new and therefore less stabilized patterns of thought and conduct. These angels do contend for spiritual forms, but they are not the source of ultrasectarianism and meaningless controversial divisions of professed religionists." (See 114:6.4.)

The next major step in the reconciliation enterprise between the *UB* and the traditional church would be to bring forward the *UB*'s updated teachings of Jesus and inquire deeply as to whether they include—if anything!—aspects of today's legacy ecclesiastical systems. If there are such elements, these would be essential for "the new church." One that comes to mind is his laying on of his hands to commission his apostles. This practice could be continued, I think, because groups of people always need leaders—a fact the *UB* clearly recognizes. This gesture could certainly be retained as a simple way of providing guidance in Christ-centered communities of every kind. In addition, the Jesus of *The Urantia Book* clearly implemented one particular sacrament, called the "Remembrance Supper." (See 179:5.6.) Urantians might also argue that there are other such "ecclesiastical" elements in the Lord's updated teachings provided in the *UB* that might overlap with past church practice.

The Role of Cultural Facts in the Life of the Church

I've recently come to believe that most of the ecclesiastical systems of traditional Christianity have to do with fulfilling many of the simple religious needs people have. It also seems likely that the Lord "fosters" these things for that very purpose. We might even say that these church practices have been inspired by the Spirit of Truth and can be accepted as part of the Lord's plan for helping his followers to grow in his love.

These ecclesiastical elements are too numerous to mention: liturgy, the priesthood, canonizations, praying to the saints, sacraments, statuary, Mariology, eschatology, pilgrimages, and so on. One of the geniuses of Catholicism is that it understands the religious desires of people and seeks to meet those needs. It does not base the claims of its system—at least not all of them!— on the idea that "this is what the Lord founded." On some of them she does; on many not. I don't think the *UB* can be cited as an authority for all of them, or even most of them, but likely for some of them.

In this connection, I have come across the helpful concept of a "cultural fact." Some rites or practices or traditions may not technically be true historically speaking, nor are they easily traceable back to scripture; however, they have been *believed* to be so, and thus have become a part of the general belief system of the church. It is now a "cultural fact." I find this concept helpful in our enterprise of transition to the future.

In other words, most of the beliefs and practices of the church, if we take the *UB* as our final authority, are really cultural facts. We as Urantians might justifiably declare that the Spirit of Truth has fostered them and that they have been shown over centuries to support genuine faith. If some people no longer believe in them, well, this is not a great loss as these cultural facts really do lack historical or scriptural foundation. This is happening a great deal today and probably always has happened.

The label "cultural fact" would even apply to some of the dogmatic teachings of the church, but not all of them. Some of them, including key features of the Chalcedonian Creed, were legitimate developments of doctrine that correspond to *UB* teaching—for example, the Creed's doctrines of the Trinity and the divinity of Christ, including its definition of his dual nature.[163]

Consider also our Mariology. On one hand, it should be obvious that much of Mariology comprises cultural facts, including the dogma of the virgin birth. But on the other hand, the profound sophiology of modern Russian theologians such as Soloviev, Bulgakov, and Florensky could easily be applied to the *UB*'s revelations about the existence of the Mother Spirit, the co-equal deity consort of Jesus Christ as revealed especially in Paper 34, "The Local Universe Mother Spirit." I think these Russian thinkers really had an insight into her reality and attributes, as did some of the writers of the Gnostic gospels. Once the natural birth of the Lord is accepted in light of the *UB*'s detailed narration about the nativity, then much of our over-blown Mariology could

---

[163] Urantians do not believe that Christ Michael *was himself literally the Second Person of the Trinity*. I think the *UB* is somewhat Arian in this sense, and this will be one of the major criticisms against *UB*. The *UB* is also Gnostic or Platonic in its teaching about emanations from the Paradise Trinity. Some of the old Gnostics had valid intuitions in this regard. It will have to be shown that the *UB* is in some sense Gnostic, but that these features can now be reconciled with Christianity. In the early centuries they couldn't achieve this reconciliation, but the *UB* now provides the revelation required to partially justify these ancient heresies. It must also be made clear that while Gnosticism said salvation consisted in knowing these theories and *not* in faith in Jesus, *UB* teaches that the new life consists in faith in Jesus and in that sense is *not* Gnostic.

be replaced by the above sophiological theories. As well, much of our present Mariology could be applied to the *UB*'s authoritative new revelation of the Holy Mother Spirit. I also think that, practically speaking, Mary now serves in this role in the minds of traditional Christians who believe in her; certainly in the worship of most Catholic and Orthodox believers she has this function.

The Appealing Eschatology of the *UB*

Much of our current eschatologies are cultural facts too, and would have to be revised in light of the *UB*.[164] A lot needs to be done in this field. In fact, I believe the teachings of the *UB* on eschatology will be one of the most appealing and the least contentious aspects of our transition project. Our existing Christian eschatology is by all accounts very poor and primitive. For example, the great Catholic theologian Hans Urs von Balthasar said about life after death that we know absolutely nothing! The eschatology in the *UB* can be readily accepted because how can the Church disagree with what she knows nothing about?

Nor do I see anything in the *UB*'s eschatology that goes strongly against present teaching. For example, its concept of the spiritual (morontia) body; the idea of universal resurrection on the "mansion worlds" after death; its teaching about continuing growth in an eternal afterlife; and so on. It's all so beautiful and hopeful! The eschatology of the *UB* is simply far above and beyond our present understanding.

I should add that many of the NDE or life-after-life experiences being widely reported today also correspond to *UB* eschatology, including the depictions of merciful judgment based on records kept by angels and what is laid down in the soul itself. And I think before long we will discover life on other planets as described in some detail in the *UB*. (See Paper 49, "The Inhabited Worlds.") Maybe one of the UFOs will even land and its occupants talk with us! This is part of eschatology too, in that it would be one indicator of the end of Urantia's quarantine because of the Lucifer rebellion.

---

[164] Please see in this connection chapter 15 in this book, "Do All Ascenders Survive?"

Preserving Continuities *and* Discontinuities

So, my approach is that I would emphasize these two elements: first, the idea that Christ's teaching is very simple and probably devoid of any real ecclesiastical structure, and second, that the Holy Spirit has fostered many aspects of the church to fulfill the real needs of the growing community. I would emphasize that this latter aspect is part of the will of Christ—again, because of his compassionate recognition of the religious needs of regular people.

Another aspect of the genius of Catholicism is that she is really open for her members to live a great variety of life-styles and spiritualities. If you want to, you can live like a Shaker without any liturgy or obedience to clergy—as long as you do not say that this is the *only way*, and as long as you don't contend that we don't need all the "cultural facts" of Catholicism that are there, frankly, to support less spiritual people!

It should be remembered that the radical reformers of the Reformation saw their approach as the *only* authentic gospel way. As a result, they threw out all the other methods people traditionally used in seeking God—including the seven sacraments or the ancient practice throughout Christendom of monasticism, for example. Millions of people worldwide belong to the Catholic or Orthodox Church because it fulfills their ordinary religious needs through these things.

One of the most crucial aspects of the great transition will be *for the clergy* to accept that what they do may indeed be part of what the Lord "fosters," but may not in the end be essential for Christian life. This is why, in my view, we are talking about *a few centuries* for this entire enterprise. Gradually the clergy and many sincerely devout people will have to be weaned off many of the "cultural facts" and be called instead to the simplicity of the teaching of Christ. We would, at that time, have centuries of tradition to guide us. People could be allowed to still use cultural facts if so needed, but those who are the more progressive teachers would always be trying to lead believers to a deeper life in Christ without so many cultural trappings. We even do that now.

It is worth emphasizing that the radical sects of the Reformation didn't think Luther had gone far enough. Some of these sects did not go as far as the Christ of *UB*, but some of them did. I think we can learn a lot from them about separating the essence of Christ's religion from the mass of cultural facts!

However, what most of these radical reformers did not appreciate was that the church supplied real needs with its sacraments, religious images, pilgrimages, monastic and religious life, and so on. The extreme reformers tried to call everyone to an absolutely simple kind of gospel life that few could attain. And yet, there has always been in our mystical tradition an understanding of this simple essence of the gospel, and many teachers and prophets have historically called people to turn deeply within. It is certainly a large trend today. The greatest wisdom, I think, would be to keep pursuing this mystical call to ultimate simplicity *in union with* serving the normal religious needs of ordinary people.

Indeed, for decades and centuries to come it should be emphasized that one does not have to leave traditional Christianity and the legacy church in order to follow the Christ of the *UB*. Adherents of *The Urantia Book*'s teachings need to acquire the humility of Christ who allowed his closest followers to continue with their Jewish practices even in his own lifetime.

Today's ecclesiastical systems of Catholicism and Orthodoxy foster faith to an enormous degree in people. I think one of the real dangers of an exclusive *UB* approach to Christ is that it becomes another *ideology* and doesn't really foster faith as much as the traditional ecclesiastical systems do. The *UB* and its current gatherings can become very abstract and even dissociated. The Urantia revelation's advocates can certainly learn a great deal from traditional Christianity even as they endeavor to correct its errors and excesses.

The Urantia Revelation and the Problem of Evil

Byron Belitsos

This essay is adapted from chapter 8 of Truths about Evil, Sin, and the Demonic: Toward an Integral Theodicy for the Twenty-first Century *(Wipf & Stock, 2023). It compares the Christian theological treatment of the "problem of evil," technically known as "theodicy," to that provided in the Urantia revelation.*

A scripture typically serves as a trustworthy reference text that supports research, reflection, and worship. *The Urantia Book* functions in this way for scientifically literate and philosophically inclined spiritual seekers who are adventurous enough to plunge into this demanding work. The *UB*'s American readers often start out "post-Christian" but soon fall in love with the book's depiction of Jesus, and many find themselves with renewed interest in the Bible as a secondary reference text.

The *UB* does not lay out an explicit theodicy in a single paper or section, but its focus on the problem of evil is clearly manifest across the entire text. In this chapter I assemble some of its key statements pertaining to theodicy under three major categories: the problem of moral freedom; the possible levels of moral "turpitude"; and the factor of angelology and cosmology.

We'll first begin with premises. Significantly for our discussion of theodicy, the *UB* teaches that the human mind is morally positive. The normal human mind, it declares—reminiscent of the philosopher

Immanuel Kant[165]—naturally manifests a *positive intuition of moral duty*.

Further, the *UB* declares that "the psychology of a child is naturally positive. . . . In the absence of wrong teaching, the mind of the normal child moves positively." [166]

This in-born intuitive capacity has a *cosmic* basis. It corresponds to what the *UB* calls the "judicial form of cosmic discrimination." This God-given ability to recognize fairness and fitness in interpersonal relationships is one part of a trio of mind capacities revealed in the *UB* that includes two other non-moral forms of intuition. These three intuitions, by divine design, are innate in all human minds.[167]

Stated otherwise, an a priori sense of moral duty is foundational according to the *UB*. As the child matures, these impulses are incrementally upgraded by the more advanced leadings of the Indwelling Spirit, the God-bestowed entity that is comparable to the ancient Greek term *pneuma*, the "inner light" of Quakerism, the *atman* of Hinduism, or Buddha's teaching about the *Buddha-nature*. The Indwelling Spirit, we are told, is bestowed by God the Father at about age six to all normal-minded children in response to the child's first other-directed moral choice, which has made its appearance naturally.

---

[165] For Kant, the sense of moral duty is innate, or self-manifesting. Remarkably, the *UB* also fully embraces Kant's notion that there are three cardinal faculties of mind: willing, thinking, and feeling. This is distinct from the three cosmic intuitions listed in the footnote just below.

[166] *The Urantia Book*, 103:2.3. Curiously, this notion appears to echo the thought of Enlightenment thinker Jean-Jacques Rousseau, who famously pronounced that an inclination to moral goodness is preponderant in the normal child, but is perverted by social norms. His opponent Thomas Hobbes held that men are "naturally wicked," but Rousseau argued that "uncorrupted morals" prevail in the state of nature, an idea later embraced by the Romantic movement.

[167] *Moral duty* is one of "three cosmic intuitions" that comprise an intrinsic "reality sensitivity" present in all humans. The *UB* defines this form of intuition as "*duty*—the reality domain of morals in the philosophic realm, the arena of reason, the recognition of relative right and wrong." The other two innate intuitions are (1) the *mathematical* and (2) *reverential* forms of cosmic discrimination. These intuitions are "constitutive in the self-consciousness of reflective thinking" (*The Urantia Book*, 16:6).

From this point forward, the Indwelling Spirit presents moral options (in unobtrusive ways) to surface consciousness. It gently endeavors to "adjust" the human thought process with its infallible leadings, but its success in reaching us is always subject to human choice.

In normal circumstances, the Spirit slowly prevails. Because of this divine endowment—which we are told is a fragment of the infinite God—the possible degrees of positive moral action according to the *UB* are unlimited. We can and will rise ever-higher in the scale of moral attainment, quite literally forever, in our eternal afterlife. Each willing person progresses in an endless journey of increasingly more advanced moral, intellectual, social, and spiritual achievements. In my view, the *UB*'s story of this adventure is easily the most detailed elucidation of the afterlife in the world's religious literature.

At some point in this afterlife journey we achieve "God-fusion" (irrevocable identification with the Indwelling Spirit), and eons later we attain actual perfection.[168]

The self-perfecting adventure of our ascension to Paradise entails the traversal of several hundred stages of advancement. We move "inward and upward" through ever more advanced training and socialization experiences on higher-dimensional worlds, after which we "graduate" from the space-time universe and begin the grand voyage through the perfect worlds of Havona in the eternal central universe. After this stupendous experience we move inward to Paradise itself, the very source of all things and beings, and in this most exalted domain we achieve what is known as *finaliter* status, which signifies our attainment of ultimate perfection. Thereupon we are assigned to advanced duties throughout the inhabited material universes. And then, after all this "perfection training" is completed, we are later dispatched to the

---

[168] One thinks of this classic passage: "Be perfect, therefore, as your heavenly Father is perfect" (Matthew 5:48). The *UB* offers a variety of renditions, such as: "From the Universal Father who inhabits eternity there has gone forth the supreme mandate, 'Be you perfect, even as I am perfect'" (1:0.3). Attributed to Jesus: "Be merciful, even as God is merciful, and in the eternal future of the kingdom you shall be perfect, even as your heavenly Father is perfect" (140.3.14).

galaxies of the "outer universes" to take on unrevealed responsibilities in domains that are currently uninhabited.[169]

I. Distinguishing True from False Liberty

Back on earth, the foundational God-given ability to discriminate right from wrong launches the great ascent. But down here, of course, one must consider nurture as well as nature. In addition, we inherit amoral animal-origin survival instincts that are deeply rooted in our biology. As these biological and environmental factors intermingle uneasily with our divine endowments of relative free will and moral discrimination, we have a sure formula for trouble as well as opportunity.

What happens, then, if an extremely adverse social environment prevails in the early life of a growing child? We can anticipate that a traumatized mind and a depraved sense of self may overwhelm the innate sense of positive moral duty.

Worse, this condition may obliterate the impact of higher spiritual influences (as depicted, for example, in the Catholic concept of deadly sin discussed below). A grossly self-centered child or one that is emotionally disturbed, as it grows to adulthood, might well turn to "license"—i.e., the wildly unregulated misuse of a free will bent on exploitative relationships or self-destructive pursuits.

According to the *UB*, dark influences can unleash illusions of *false liberty*, which it defines as profligate willing based on fear, addiction, and self-aggrandizement. The allures of false liberty can at some point destroy our natural predisposition to goodness—that is, our innate desire to do good to others as we would to ourselves. The *UB* calls this moral stance *true liberty*.

False liberty creates chaos and leads to bondage. True liberty entails balancing respect for the rights of others with the rights of self accord

---

[169] "The mortal finaliters have fully complied with the injunction of the ages, 'Be you perfect'; they have ascended the universal path of mortal attainment; they have found God, and they have been duly inducted into the Corps of the Finality. Such beings have attained the present limit of spirit progression but not *finality of ultimate spirit status*. They have achieved the present limit of creature perfection but not *finality of creature service*. They have experienced the fullness of Deity worship but not *finality of experiential Deity attainment*" (*The Urantia Book*, 31:3.6).

to the Golden Rule. The *UB* organizes these ideas in systematic form in these rich passages, with my emphasis added:

> True liberty is progressively related to reality and is ever regardful of social equity, cosmic fairness, universe fraternity, and divine obligations. *Liberty is suicidal when divorced from material justice, intellectual fairness, social forbearance, moral duty, and spiritual values.* Liberty is nonexistent apart from cosmic reality . . . Unbridled self-will and unregulated self-expression equal unmitigated selfishness, the acme of ungodliness. . . . License masquerading in the garments of liberty is the forerunner of abject bondage. . . .True liberty is the associate of genuine self-respect; false liberty is the consort of self-admiration.

> *True liberty is the fruit of self-control; false liberty, the assumption of self-assertion.* Self-control leads to altruistic service; self-admiration tends towards the exploitation of others for the selfish aggrandizement of such a mistaken individual as is willing to sacrifice righteous attainment for the sake of possessing unjust power over his fellow beings.[170]

Is the attainment of genuine liberty, or true righteousness, solely the product of a person's intuitive apprehension of the rights of self and others? This sort of righteous discernment is necessary but not sufficient for rapid advancement, according to the revelators. This is because faith in God's abiding goodness, and the effort to engage in frequent communion with this loving God, is also essential in the equation. We must have been "born of the spirit."

Curiously, the Jesus of the Urantia revelation preaches a modified version of the Lutheran doctrine of righteousness through faith. In a sermon called "Lesson on Self-Mastery," he alludes to prophet Jeremiah's teaching that "the human heart is deceitful above all things and sometimes even desperately wicked."[171] A regressive, animal-origin

---

[170] Both quotes from *The Urantia Book*, 54:1.3–6.

[171] *The Urantia Book*, 143:2.5.

tendency is naturally present, Jesus goes on to say, in those who are not yet "saved by faith" and regenerated in the spirit. This phrasing makes subtle reference to Luther (and Paul), and thus may be using them as "human sources"—even as the text negates other Reformation doctrines such as original sin and predestination.[172]

Also remarkably, the *UB* affirms the Bible's cosmic-conflict framework, its depiction of a "war in heaven" between Christ and Satan. This is laid out in the *UB*'s unprecedented revelations about the Lucifer Rebellion provided in Papers 53, 54, and 67. It makes clear that *systematic sin*, that is—the defiant and persistent practice of unmitigated selfishness—occupies a moral category all its own and derives from external sources. It may be surprising to many to learn that the Urantia revelation validates the ancient premise that "demonic" supernatural influences have deeply affected the course of human evolution.

No doubt the human heart can become "desperately wicked" on its own. But a key theodical teaching of the Urantia Revelation is that organized, deliberate evil, while always possible without off-planet interference in human affairs, entered into our world in pre-historic times with overwhelming force because of iniquitous *non-human* sources.

Once such an influence is imported by powerful higher-dimensional beings, these dark presences can easily prey upon and magnify our own built-in human tendency toward false liberty. And when these miscreants collaborate, directly or indirectly, with power-hungry human elites, this can lead to frequent eruptions of horrendous events. This factor appears to be a major source or cause of such demonic evils.

---

[172] Tenets of Luther's core doctrine of justification were taught by Jesus as depicted in the *UB*, for example in this passage, with emphasis added: *"Salvation is by the regeneration of the spirit and not by the self-righteous deeds of the flesh. You are justified by faith* and fellowshipped by grace, not by fear and the self-denial of the flesh, albeit the Father's children who have been born of the spirit are ever and always *masters* of the self and all that pertains to the desires of the flesh. When you know that you are *saved by faith*, you have real peace with God." A few paragraphs later the sermon seems to allude to Luther again: "Even this saving faith you have not of yourselves; *it [your faith] also is the gift of God.* And if you are the children of this living faith, *you are no longer the bondslaves of self* but rather the triumphant masters of yourselves, the liberated sons of God" (*The Urantia Book*, 143:2.6–8).

St. Augustine also held that the radical perversion of human free will was in part a privation caused in part by external forces, specifically by fallen angels who corrupted Adam and Eve. The *UB* ratifies this general idea, but entirely reframes the old mythic discourse with a revealed narrative of planetary pre-history embedded in a scientific cosmology that is supported by a plethora of modern philosophic distinctions.

II. The Spectrum of Moral Turpitude

The righteous exercise of liberty leads to (and is based on) self-control and self-respect and results in loving relationships, enlightened citizenship, and creative living. But the misuse of free will can lead to a descending sequence of increasingly destructive behaviors that can be laid out along a spectrum that allows us to classify the type of immorality according to the intent of the perpetrator, among other factors. Along this scale we witness increasing levels of defiance against "recognized reality," to use the *UB*'s operative phrase, and a decreasing ability to repent and repair damaged relationships.

Traditional Christianity tends to identify any negative behavior as "sin," perhaps to drive home the pervasiveness of original sin. Catholic moral teaching breaks this out further as the seven deadly sins (or cardinal sins) that "destroy the grace of God in the heart of the sinner": pride, greed, lust, envy, gluttony, wrath, and sloth.[173] This teaching was later passed down to mainline Protestant denominations relatively intact.[174]

---

[173] A list of seven virtues also corresponds to the cardinal sins: *humility, charity, chastity, gratitude, temperance, patience, and diligence.*

[174] Some historians believe that the practice of listing the types of sins originated from the monastic tradition of early Christian Egypt, which identified nine *logismoi* (a term introduced in chapter 3). This list was modified and codified by the Catholic Church by the sixth century. The *UB* strongly agrees with the wider Christian tradition that pride (the first item listed) is the most damaging of the vices: "Of all the dangers which beset man's mortal nature and jeopardize his spiritual integrity, pride is the greatest. Courage is valorous, but egotism is vainglorious and suicidal. Reasonable self-confidence is not to be deplored. Man's ability to transcend himself is the one thing which distinguishes him from the animal kingdom. Pride is deceitful, intoxicating, and sin-breeding whether found in an individual, a group, a race, or a nation. It is literally true, 'Pride goes before a fall'" (*The Urantia Book*, 111:6.9-10).

The broad Christian tradition tends to emphasize types rather than levels of immorality, but Catholic catechisms also distinguish deadly sins from venial sins, transgressions committed with less self-awareness of wrong-doing.[175]

The Urantia Revelation provides more focus on levels or stages of moral self-awareness. It adds clarity by spelling out, at least according to my interpretation, a graduated scale of four categories of negative moral choice along with its own "typology of faults," as I put it (which is not explicit but rather inferred in the course of my discussion below). The *UB* contrasts this list with positive gradations that range from the dawn of moral sensitivity in early childhood to the achievement of moral perfection far into the afterlife.

A philosophic description of the negative side of the spectrum is attributed to Jesus, in a dialogue with Apostle Thomas during a sojourn in Galilee:

> Evil is the unconscious or unintended transgression of the divine law, the Father's will. Evil is likewise the measure of the imperfectness of obedience to the Father's will. Sin is the conscious, knowing, and deliberate transgression of the divine law, the Father's will. Sin is the measure of unwillingness to be divinely led and spiritually directed. Iniquity is the willful, determined, and persistent transgression of the divine law, the Father's will.[176]

A more systematic teaching is provided in Paper 54, entitled "Problems of the Lucifer Rebellion":

---

[175] Philosopher of religion John Hick has complained about imprecise language regarding the nature of evil or levels of evildoing: In French, for example, *le mal* refers to any sort of evil action, and the German term *Ubel* stands for moral evil in general and even natural evil. Adding to the confusion, says Hick, is that "the Augustinian tradition of theodicy, on its more philosophical side, traces all other evils, moral and natural, back to [metaphysical evil] as their ultimate cause or occasion." This move seems to miss the point, Hick convincingly argues, since metaphysical evil refers to the inherent finitude of the created universe, which is not easily translated into a spectrum of moral categories. (See Hick, *Evil and the God of Love*, 12–14.)

[176] *The Urantia Book*, 148:4.3.

The Gods neither create evil or permit sin and rebellion. Potential evil is time-existent in a universe embracing differential levels of perfection meanings and values. Sin is potential in all realms where imperfect beings are endowed with the ability to choose between good and evil. The very conflicting presence of truth and untruth, fact and falsehood, constitutes the potentiality of error. The deliberate choice of evil constitutes sin [and] the persistent pursuit of sin and error is iniquity.[177]

Allow me to restate these passages in more practical terms, along with my own typology of faults:

Error: At the more or less innocent end of the spectrum we find honest mistakes born of ignorance and inexperience. I categorize these as perspectival faults that arise from youth, immaturity, or defective education. Such folks lack proper perspective on their moral choices, and are willing to correct their errors after experiencing painful consequences or when offered moral instruction.

Evil: Behavior can turn incrementally darker if one's values and intentions are not clarified by personal reflection informed by wholehearted faith. Intuitions of moral duty arise spontaneously in a normal mind; meditation and prayer can make these ideas more apparent, and periods of stillness or worship refresh and enhance the pathways of moral insight. But without firm intention and commitment, this subtle input is easy to ignore or marginalize, or may in worse cases be entirely obstructed by selfish craving or attachment to prejudices. Stated otherwise, the average person senses such inner impulses to do good, but those on the road to evildoing are too prideful, confused, indifferent, or slothful to bother to sort them out. They are unfocused and distracted by the clamor of wants and desires, and because they're not born of the spirit (or are backsliders), they lead lives of

---

[177] *The Urantia Book*, 54:2.

unresolved or thoughtless internal conflict. They become evil (by this definition) if they fall into *habitually* confused, distracted, or conflict-ridden behavior. Generally, evildoers are redeemable; they may feel remorse and act on it. Evil behavior manifests as *conflictual faults.*

Sin: If a person is raised without moral instruction and mired in childhood trauma, or is subjected to otherwise destructive teachings or circumstances, they may turn to rebellious behavior and deliberate evildoing, a lifestyle of "false liberty" as described earlier. "Sin is the measure of unwillingness to be divinely led and spiritually directed," as Jesus puts it in the earlier quote. While sinning easily becomes habitual or addictive, sinners are generally defined in the *UB* as those who make specific and calculated plans to carry out their transgressive deeds for the sake of self-aggrandizement, revenge, or malice, but especially pride.[178] Sins are therefore *deliberative faults.*[179]

Iniquity: In the very worst cases, some grow up to become defiant perpetrators of methodical sin who may cultivate alliances with dark forces, real or imagined. They are consciously identified with sin and darkness and often verge on mental derangement or suicide. Some people maintain their persistent sinning through grim efforts at mental compartmentalization, pathological rationalization, or

---

[178] "The courage required to effect the conquest of nature and to transcend one's self is a courage that might succumb to the temptations of self-pride. The mortal who can transcend self might yield to the temptation to deify his own self-consciousness. The mortal dilemma consists in the double fact that man is in bondage to nature while at the same time he possesses a unique liberty— freedom of spiritual choice and action. On material levels man finds himself subservient to nature, while on spiritual levels he is triumphant over nature and over all things temporal and finite. Such a paradox is inseparable from temptation, potential evil, decisional errors, and when self becomes proud and arrogant, sin may evolve" (*The Urantia Book*, 11:6.2).

[179] "Sin in time-conditioned space clearly proves the temporal liberty—even license— of the finite will. Sin depicts immaturity dazzled by the freedom of the relatively sovereign will of personality while failing to perceive the supreme obligations and duties of cosmic citizenship" (*The Urantia Book*, 118:7.4).

even assent to "mind control" by demonic forces. This of course is the lowest end of the spectrum. These folks are irredeemable and impervious to mercy. I think of the faults of iniquitous perpetrators as *systematic*.

Thus, according to the teachings of the *UB*, we can say that the gradations of moral descent extend from error, to evil, to sin, and then to iniquity (or the demonic), and these moral faults begin as *perspectival* and then worsen to become *conflictual, deliberative*, and *systematic*. In the chart below, these gradations comprise the vertical axis, and the faults are arrayed across the top.

There is one additional element to consider: The problem of accidents is difficult to classify, but is an ever-present factor on a material planet. Though not technically on the spectrum of moral action, a wide variety of chance occurrences can pose moral dilemmas. This category broadly refers to the unpredictability of natural process that are nonetheless subject to discoverable laws of physics or biology. I include this issue here also as a theological rebuttal to the omni-causal theodicies of Luther and especially Calvin, who denied the very possibility of chance events of misfortune. Everyday accidents can be a menace to all of us, but a larger threat is posed by the evolving physical mechanisms behind earthquakes, droughts, floods, hurricanes, as well as the random biological occurrence that lead to genetic defects or pandemics—traditionally the constituents of "natural evil." Mitigating human suffering from these factors is a moral challenge that calls forth disciplines such as engineering, medicine, and good government; but it is the beyond the scope of this discussion to parse out the morality of modern politics.

Below are charted the five categories that comprise the spectrum of moral negativity and four types of moral fault (as well as the likelihood of repentance).

	perspectival	conflictual	deliberative	systematic	—description—
accident					chance mishaps or random changes in natural mechanisms create pain; no moral choice is involved; suffering results, but never intended; humans can mitigate through a moral commitment to science or good governance
error	✓				poor choices resulting from ignorance, narrowness of viewpoint, or immaturity; may or may not directly cause suffering; remorse is very likely
evil	✓	✓			confused or conflicted relationship to moral values, or at worst the reckless but not systematic choice of error for self-serving reasons; remorse remains possible
sin	✓	✓	✓		deliberate rebellion against recognized values of duty, fairness, equity, fraternity; habitually engages in false liberty while knowingly causing harm; behavior frequently causes chaos and violence; repentance is not impossible, but is unlikely
iniquity	✓	✓	✓	✓	knowingly self-identified with sinful choices; methodically defiant to truth for the sake of selfish gain; premeditated malice; loss of self-control leading to soul suicide; repentance is not possible

1: The Spectrum of Moral Turpitude

Bearing these distinctions in mind, let's proceed to further inquire into the pervasive presence of iniquity on our world, which the *UB* asserts is largely due to a primeval angelic rebellion. However, there is a prerequisite: To better understand this rebellion's import, we will need to know something about the cosmology that supports this bleak narrative.

III. Corrections Regarding Cosmology and Angelology

Much of our confusion about the mystery of evil is due to the archaic worldviews that accompany our scriptures. And that's a key reason why the authors of the *UB* engage in such an enormous effort to address our outdated and inadequate ideas about cosmology, angelology, the afterlife, and the epochal events of our pre-history. The *UB*'s teachings on these topics are essential for grasping its discussion of the problem of evil and, in turn, its integrative theodicy. As part of this effort at correction, the *UB*'s cosmology depicts what might be called a *dialectical multiverse*. I'll break this model down into the three aspects (among many) that most contribute to our discussion of theodicy:

1. *Key features of the multiverse*: Until the twentieth century, the context for Christian theodicy had been a geocentric and later a heliocentric single-planet cosmology. The earth was the charge of angels and deities residing in the heavenly realm just "above." At heaven's highest level was the God-man Jesus Christ, Creator and savior, along with two coequal members of the Eternal Trinity. In far distant times, according to vague biblical passages, one portion of the angels of heaven had rebelled against Christ. We read that they were "thrown down" as a result of his visitation to earth and were awaiting final judgment.

By contrast, twenty-first century discoveries confront us with hard evidence of several trillion galaxies and the prospect of innumerable inhabited planets, and it is fair to assert that the UB anticipated this current picture by seventy years. But the Urantia material also adds a revealed depiction of unseen dimensions with higher worlds described in rational language stripped of fanciful trappings. Generally speaking, it describes an evolving multiverse with seven trillion inhabited planets ministered to by numerous orders of higher beings operating across seven great galactic divisions called "superuniverses."

What makes this multiverse dialectical? As noted earlier, perfect citizens populate the central universe (along with a vast angelic and superangelic host).[180] Almost unfathomable to us, these beings have been present from eternity in this, the "seventh heaven" that encircles Paradise, the perfect "residence" of the Deities. While these denizens of heaven are forever perfect, we are told that they are in dialectical and complemental relationship with the *perfecting* citizens of the evolving universes who are slowly ascending to the central universe wherein they can personally attain the finality of perfection and ultimate fulfillment. The architecture of the universe, for our limited purposes, therefore comprises (1) the eternal central universe of perfection and (2) the vast evolutional realms of perfecting ascenders known as the grand universe. And thus its is fair to say that time and eternity, change and changelessness, perfection and the imperfection—these opposing dimensions of the multiverse—subsist in a polar or dialectical relationship, much as envisioned by Christian philosopher Charles Hartshorne. With regard to the problem of evil and adversity, this statement sums up the "design concept" of our dialectical multiverse:

> The confusion and turmoil of Urantia do not signify that the Paradise Rulers lack either interest or ability to manage affairs differently. The Creators are possessed of full power to make Urantia a veritable paradise, but such an Eden would not contribute to the development of those strong, noble, and experienced characters which the Gods are so surely forging out on your world between the anvils of necessity and the hammers of anguish. Your anxieties and sorrows, your trials and disappointments, are just as much a part of the divine plan on your sphere as are the exquisite perfection

---

[180] Prominent religious philosopher Alvin Plantinga has envisioned that among the "many worlds" possible, one such world would be a moral utopia. If we can believe the *UB*, not only can we envision in theory an ideal world in which every creature freely and consistently chooses the good; the central universe truly *is* such a utopia. This may also illustrate Augustine's "principle of plenitude" according to which, if God desired this possibility to become actual as one expression of divine glory, it would certainly come into being.

and infinite adaptation of all things to their supreme purpose on the worlds of the central and perfect universe.[181]

2. *Local universe administration*: The *UB* teaches that the Trinity operates (or self-distributes) in the grand universe through the vehicle of subordinate deities and administrators. At the level that most concerns us, the Trinity directly personalizes as "local" Creators (of which there are 700,000 across the myriads of inhabited galaxies). We are told: "One of the greatest sources of confusion on Urantia concerning the nature of God grows out of the failure of your sacred books clearly to distinguish . . . between Paradise Deity and the local universe Creators and administrators."[182]

The Creator of our local universe, called *Nebadon*, incarnated on earth as Jesus Christ, we are taught in the *UB*, but is *not* the literal Second Person of the Trinity. (Nebadon contains 3,840,101 inhabited planets and will eventually have 10,000,000 inhabited worlds.) He was directly created by (or "stems from") the Eternal Son and Universal Father on Paradise, and he repletely expresses their deity characteristics in and for his local creation. That is why "He who has seen the Son has seen the Father" (John 14:9).

And yet there is another surprising distinction. Christ Michael was created on Paradise alongside a co-equal feminine deity. As his divine consort, she perfectly expresses the Third Person of the Trinity, the Infinite Spirit, and thus the two together represent the Trinity to our local universe. She is known as the *Universe Mother Spirit*, and is the Creator of the vast orders of ministering angels. She is also the very source of life itself and of our mind endowment as such. But the take-home here is that these two are created beings who themselves

---

[181] *The Urantia Book*, 23:2.12.

[182] See *The Urantia Book*, 4:5. This statement refers to one of three "erroneous ideas of God" found in Christian theology according to the *UB*. The other two are the "blood atonement" doctrine and the failure "clearly to distinguish between the personalities of the Paradise Trinity." Allow me to restate the third of these three fallacies about God: a lack of understanding of the distinction between *evolutional deities* resident in the evolving universes and *existential deity* residing in the eternal domains. (See 4:5.)

are sub-absolute Creators, and indeed they are our immediate Creator Parents.[183]

I provide all this detail and context to help us better understand the predicament of theodicy on earth: We are told that the chief celestial minister to our *local system* of one thousand planets, an "administrative angel" named *Lucifer*, led a system-wide rebellion against the local universe government of Christ Michael and Mother Spirit. It was Michael's charge to confront Lucifer's agents on our world and to de facto terminate the rebellion; Michael's consort, the Universe Mother, along with her angels of many orders, provided essential support for this complex mission. For examples, see Mark 4:11: "Then the devil left him, and behold, angels came and were ministering to him" and Luke 22:41: "He withdrew about a stone's throw beyond them, knelt down and prayed [and] an angel from heaven appeared to him and strengthened him."

3. *Dispensations on a normal planet compared to a rebellion world*: Ongoing human evolution on our world (or on any planet) is punctuated by epochal visitations from off-planet divine teachers and high ministers. We are told that normal planets go through seven such dispensations and that each new era is inaugurated by such superb beings. The steps of planetary progression begin with evolution of life leading to the appearance of primitive man and then proceeds over many thousands of years until a planet arrives at its far-distant destiny: the settled status of permanent planetary enlightenment called the *Era of Light and Life*. These seven epochal events on each world are of two types: (1) visitations of "Sons" of the local Creators (discussed a bit later) and (2) spectacular incarnations of Paradise-origin beings such as Christ who are sent to initiate new dispensations of planetary life and gently press

---

[183] This pair is both divine *and* evolutional. They create and rule local universes with a love and mercy that reflects the Paradise Trinity from whom they take origin. Operating as coequal male and female deity complements, they carve out local universes of millions of inhabitable worlds. They were specifically "sent out from Paradise" to populate and settle a portion of space in the evolving realms. The divine charter of such deity pairs in each of the thousands of local universes is to act as sovereign Creators, life-givers, and ministers to all life in their realms, including the creation and governance of subordinate ministers and administrators.

human evolution forward until each planet establishes a sustainable high civilization.

Sadly, two local universe "Sons,"[184] (i.e. Adam and Eve) who came to earth defaulted because of the rebellion, and these dramatic stories have heretofore remained largely unrevealed on our world. Plus, the visitation of Jesus ended in his ignominious murder, although he ultimately triumphed despite the agony of the cross. Because of these and other calamities, our world's problem in this regard is acute: We are "a full *dispensation* and more *behind* the average planetary schedule."[185] We also read:

> Urantia is not proceeding in the normal order. Your world is out of step in the planetary procession. . . . Even on normal evolutionary worlds the realization of the world-wide brotherhood of man is not an easy accomplishment. On a confused and disordered planet like Urantia such an achievement requires a much longer time and necessitates far greater effort. Unaided social evolution can hardly achieve such happy results on a spiritually isolated sphere. Religious revelation is essential to the realization of brotherhood on Urantia.[186]

---

[184] These are divine beings who were created for specific purposes by our local universe Creators, Michael and Mother Spirit.

[185] *The Urantia Book*, 52:3.7.

[186] *The Urantia Book*, 52:6.2.

15

Do All Ascenders Survive?
A Comparative Study

Reverend James Thomas (pseudonymous)
with Byron Belitsos

*The UB does not teach "universal salvation," but rather conditional
immortality. In this essay, Rev. Thomas, a Catholic priest and
monastic, explicates the controversial idea that survivors who refuse
God's plan for their ascension will be taken out of existence—with
their agreement. He explains how this concept is in harmony with
an emergent view among pioneering Catholic thinkers and some
Protestants, albeit much more detail is provided in the Urantia text.*

The traditional Catholic doctrine about hell is that it exists, is eternal, involves unending suffering, and begins at the moment of
death for all who die in the state of mortal sin. This traditional view has
its roots, of course, in Saint Augustine, one of the four original Doctors of the Church. The punishments of hell are vividly described in
his masterwork *City of God* (426), along with his other teachings about
salvation and the afterlife. Because Augustine's views have been dominant in Western Christianity ever since, the idea that unregenerate
sinners meet this fate became a key tenet of the church's eschatology—
that is, its doctrine of the "last things" or the traditional concept of our
final judgment and destiny after death. As a Catholic priest and monk,
I joined other Catholics in believing this church doctrine for most of
my life. The Catholic Church has always taught that scripture attests to
the Augustinian view in its many references to "hell" (or *Gehenna*) and

its teachings about God's wrath against sinners. However, in recent times some notable theologians, both Catholic and Protestant, have advocated at least two alternate views of final judgment, one of which is strongly supported by the eschatological teachings of *The Urantia Book*.

It is little known that these two minority approaches have roots in earlier centuries. The most prominent of these is known as *universalism*, the idea that all will eventually be saved—a teaching usually associated with Origen of Alexandria (185–253 CE). Along my Catholic way I had heard mention of Origen's teaching that everyone, even the greatest of sinners, would eventually be saved by the overpowering love of God. Also, like most Catholics, I believed that Origen's view had been condemned as a heresy. It fact, it wasn't, and it's even enjoying a revival today.

The other alternative school of thought, known as *conditionalism* or *annihilationism*, holds the view that unrepentant sinners, once they are judged, are rendered "as if they never were" in accord with their own choice and along with the assent of their divine judges. *Conditionalism* is not only upheld by the *UB*, but its roots date even further back than Origen because of numerous passages in the Old and New Testament that are often ignored.

My beliefs began to change when I first read Hans Urs von Balthasar's *Dare We Hope That All Men Be Saved* (1988). This influential Catholic theologian argues that it is acceptable to *hope* that everyone could be saved. His willingness to question Augustine led me for the first time to seriously consider universalism. My subsequent investigation, which led to my first book, turned me into a universalist. I remained one for several years until I learned more about the third alternative to both universalism and hell, which is also often called *conditional immortality*.

One of the crucial questions in eschatology is this: Can a final decision against the Father's will ever be made by his creatures? Strict universalists answer "no," and for a while this became my own answer. But later I came across the reply of the conditionalists: "Yes it is possible to make such a decision, but the result is not hell but annihilation—the utter withdrawal of one's existence." Below I share the major reasons that convinced me to become a conditionalist. However, the heart of this piece is that annihilationism is the position also taught by the Urantia revelation.

In this essay I'll first cover the universalist teaching about the possibility of a final choice; then the views of the contemporary conditionalists by comparison; and finally, that of the *UB*. I will conclude by showing how the *UB* provides the same general answer as that given by today's conditionalists, but supplements this view with more insight and information about the afterlife than has heretofore been revealed.

What Universalists Teach About the Afterlife

For the purposes of this brief paper I am only interested in one major aspect of universalism: that God's children are constitutionally *unable* to make an irrevocable decision against their Creator. This view is of course at radical variance with the major premise of conditionalism. I changed from being a universalist to a conditionalist mostly because I became convinced that such a final tragic choice not only *is* but *must* be possible. This section summarizes the main arguments of universalists against this possibility and focuses especially on the universalist premise that human freedom cannot logically take priority over the efficacy of God's grace.

We first turn to John Kronen and Eric Reitan, two distinguished philosophers who strongly oppose the traditionalist view of hell. In *God's Final Victory* (Bloomsbury Academic, 2013), they assert that God can grant what is known as "efficacious grace" to anyone he pleases, and that such acts of grace should be understood as an unearned gift that has the power to convert unrepentant souls without violating their freedom. They argue further that it is not theologically unsound for the Christian God to do this, even if this gift directly overturns the beliefs of the creature. Using intricate arguments derived from St. Thomas Aquinas and Thomas Talbott (a leading modern universalist theologian), Kronen and Reitan conclude that "God doing this [i.e., granting efficacious grace] certainly is metaphysically possible, and within God's power. [Hence] it follows that any rational creature presented with the vision of God will freely but inevitably respond affirmatively to the promise of loving union."[187] Aquinas also believed God can reveal to the unregenerate that he is their *summum bonum*, thus eliminating affective states that prevent their acceptance of his grace and mercy. And yet, Aquinas held to a complex position; he still believed it is *possible* to freely reject God, thus implicity supporting the conditionalists.

On the empirical side of things, the arguments of universalists seem to be corroborated by the contemporary reports of near-death experiencers. Many of these men and women began as agnostics or atheists. But in case after case, they experienced profound conversions upon returning from encounters in which they were apparently showered with efficacious grace.

Critics of universalism similarly argue that a sinner's bad habits or erroneous beliefs certainly *can* be changed, but they are not *necessarily* overcome in all cases by God's merciful intervention. An implacably resistant person may still be unable or simply unwilling to receive God's restorative energies, regardless of their beauty and power. For the conditionalists, then, the human will is logically prior to all other factors; it always remains possible to impede any degree of grace that is offered. The creature may successfully resist the Creator's invitation to conversion.

But universalists like Kronin and Reitan disagree: "Even if we can decide to block the vision of God by, as it were, deliberately averting our gaze, the notion of the creature as ordered to God, coupled with God's infinite causal power, seems to entail that it is within God's power to override such resistance."[188] In other words, universalists argue that it is *structurally impossible to irretrievably reject God*, a concept defended for example by Thomas Talbott in his contribution to *The Oxford Handbook on Eschatology*. Here he summarizes one of the main objections to universalism, which he defines as "some persons' willingness, despite God's best efforts to save them, to freely and finally reject God and thus separate themselves from God forever." Talbott replies with this assertion: "The New Testament picture nonetheless warrants, I believe, a stronger view, sometimes called necessary universalism: the view that

---

[187] *God's Final Victory*, 136.

[188] *God's Final Victory*, 138.

in no possible world containing created persons does God's grace fail to reconcile all of them to himself."

Conditional Immortality and the Scriptural Record

By all accounts, the ground-breaking modern book on conditional immortality is Edward Fudge's *The Fire That Consumes* (Providential Press, 1982). Fudge, a theologian and laywer, convincingly argues from the scriptural record that a sinner's systematic denial of God ultimately leads to *destruction and annihilation*—an all-consuming "fire"—rather than eternal suffering in hell or *Gehenna*.

John McKenzie, the author of *The Dictionary of the Bible* (Touchstone, 1995) and a leading biblical scholar, agrees with Fudge. Commenting on the biblical references to the word *Gehenna*, he writes: "These passages suggest that the apocalyptic imagery of other New Testament passages is to be taken for what it is, imagery, and not as strictly literal theological affirmation. The great truths of judgment and punishment are firmly retained throughout the New Testament, [but] the details of the afterlife, however, are not disclosed except in imagery."[189] In other words, scripture only offers vague *images* regarding the afterlife, rather than doctrinal statements—but at the same time we must accept as a settled scriptural truth that judgment will indeed occur after death. If we follow McKenzie's line of argument, it is not necessarily the case that the unrepentant sinner will be consigned to hell.

In fact, the leading early Apologists and Apostolic Fathers of the first few centuries read the Bible in the same way, explains Fudge. Surprisingly, none of them believed in everlasting punishment; all were conditionalists.

The key figures included many of the best-known thinkers of that era: Clement of Rome; Ignatius of Antioch; the anonymous authors of the *Didache*; Justin Martyr; and even Irenaeus. This early period of Christian thought had not yet been pervaded by the Neoplatonic concept of the immortality of the soul, an idea that captured the attention

---

[189] *The Dictionary of the Bible*, 300.

of Christian thinkers in the third century and led in a straight line to Augustine's doctrine of hell for unrepentant sinners.

Conditionalists Address the Soul's Immortality

As a Catholic growing up, my understanding was that the human soul is naturally immortal, and this remains the view of most Catholics today. However, many scholars now agree with Fudge that this view is not at all scriptural. It is in fact a "pagan" theory imported from Platonism.

But the issue is complex, according the renowned Catholic philosopher Joseph Pieper, author of *Death and Immortality* (St. Augustine's Press, 2000). Pieper distinguishes between the *indestructibility* of the soul and its *immortality*, pointing out that even Plato has been misunderstood on this subtle point.[190] Pieper clarifies the issue with a further distinction between an indestructibility that the soul has by its nature on the one hand, and the "immortality that truly conquers death" on the other.[191] This notion of indestructibility, he says, is what conditionalists also refer to as the "immortableness" of the soul—which means it is able by design to receive the gift of the resurrection or immortality from an external source. In other words, the soul naturally possesses something that makes it *capable of immortality*—"immortability" if you will. But the soul is not naturally or inherently immortal in the sense that it must eternally live on and remain self-aware, whether in heaven or in hell as taught by Augustine. Stated in terms of Christian salvation, immortality is a *gift to the soul's indestructibility* that one acquires by making a final and conscious decision for God.

Leading Catholic theologian Paul Griffiths, in his book *Decreation* (Baylor University, 2014), seems to agree with Pieper's distinction that the indestructibility of the soul allows it to survive after death. However, in this after-death state the soul is not yet a *novissimum*, that is,

---

[190] *Death and Immortality*, 77-78. "Plato himself . . . concedes that it is an inadequate use of language to call the soul 'immortal.' The established phrase 'immortality of the soul' is misleading, inasmuch as, strictly speaking, only the man but not the soul can die or not die. Hence it would be better to speak of the indestructibility of the soul, or its imperishability—as the great teachers of Christendom in fact always do."

[191] *Death and Immortality*, 80.

it has not been rendered immortal in the sense that it can never die. Its initial survival, he states, is "preliminary to something else." This something else is the final state of the soul that conditionalists would call "immortality proper," which can only be a gift of God. "The *novissimum* that is hell for human creatures may be understood as permanent and irreversible annihilation," writes Griffiths. "This condition is one of complete and final separation from the Lord. This condition amounts to success at the project of sin, which is a project of self-extrication from the Lord, who is the condition of the possibility of continuing in being for all human creatures."[192] In other words, Griffiths thinks we should keep the word "hell" but interpret it as referring to annihilation.

In the same vein, Soren Kierkegaard's classic book *Sickness unto Death* also offers a profound description of someone who is "on the way *ad nihilum*," a reflection pertinent to conditionalism. Contrary to most universalists, Kierkegaard comes down strongly on the side of *the will* being the chief cause of sin, and not intellectual ignorance. According to Kierkegaard, the Christian view is that sin resides in the will, enabling one to be defiant in an ultimate way that can lead to a tragic end: *ad nihilum*. By contrast, the universalist argument against the possibility of making a final tragic decision is based on the criterion of *ignorance*, which they believe can eventually be overcome with greater insight made possible by grace and personal revelation.

Conditionalists believe, then, that if a person consistently and unbendingly rejects the Father's will, she or he is at some point taken out of existence. Various words are used to describe this state, the most common being *annihilation*—the key term also used in *The Urantia Book* as we will soon see.

But one must ask: Is not the removal of a person from existence a terrible decision? The conditionalist replies that nonexistence is more merciful than eternal suffering. Even David Bentley Hart, a prominent Orthodox theologian and vociferous universalist, agrees with this point in his recent book *That All Shall Be Saved* (Yale University Press, 2019). He argues that "if one gives up on the idea of a hell of eternal

---

torment and poses in its place 'hell' consisting in the ultimate annihilation of evildoers at the end of days . . . admittedly the latter idea is
considerably more palatable than the former; and, for what it is worth,
it also appears to accord somewhat better with the large majority of
scriptural metaphors . . . for final damnation."[193]

On the other hand, the harsh term "annihilation" may not be the
most accurate word, as it implies a unilateral decision on God's part.
But this is not so at all, say full-fledged proponents of conditional
immortality. When a person no longer desires to fulfill the purpose of
their creation, the Lord simply *complies* with their desire; it's a mutual
decision. Because such people freely decide not to survive, and have
the power to do so, God acquiesces in their decisions albeit with profound reluctance.

The Urantia Book and the Option of Annihilation

The *UB* declares for the possibility of annihilation. Self-extinction is
available, it says, for those few who reject the "easy yoke" of divine government. These defiant and unregenerate persons—having resurrected
into the first phase of the afterlife—are not forced to embark on the
eternal ascent. Nor is some form of efficacious grace applied to forcefully overpower such iniquitous souls. They have the right to spurn
eternal life, but such a determination is possible only after competent
heavenly counselors make the stakes clear, declares the Urantia revelation. In these extreme cases, judges presiding at the highest levels of
universe government may issue a sentence of annihilation, whereupon
such a personality "becomes as though it had never been" (2:3.2).

The Urantia text is quick to add that such acts of final justice are
"always tempered with mercy"; all possible efforts are made to assure
each person—even the worst transgressors—that divine forgiveness is
readily available. Every attempt is made to motivate them to choose
survival, and the celestial judges in all cases offer the option of merciful rehabilitation. But they cannot coerce compliance with such a
sentence, thus leaving only one other option: annihilation, which
is in effect self-annihilation. Biblically, the creature's final choice for

193   *That All Shall Be Saved*, 86-87.

oblivion is known as the "second death," the eternal death that only occurs in the heavenly realm itself (cf. Revelation 21:8).

In summary, all ex-mortals either agree to a mandated rehabilitation—or else must assent to be annihilated as a purely personal and free choice; this is their binary choice once the protocols of final judgment have been exercised.

We must again emphasize that the decision for a "second death" is up to the individual: "The final result of wholehearted sin is annihilation. In the last analysis, such sin-identified individuals have destroyed themselves by becoming wholly unreal through their embrace of iniquity" (2:3.2).

And, there can be no resurrection from such a fate; it is everlasting and eternal: "Upon the cessation of life, upon cosmic dissolution, such an isolated personality is absorbed into the oversoul of creation, becoming a part of the evolving experience of the Supreme Being" (2:3.4).

I am aware that millions of modern secularists believe that such "cosmic dissolution" is their natural fate at death. But this is not the annihilation referred to in the Urantia revelation. Its teaching soars far beyond the mechanistic understanding of materialists, but it also offers a vast correction of the outworn Christian view of the afterlife. And this is due to the *UB*'s unprecedented revelations about our afterlife ascension into higher-dimensional worlds.

Oddly, the Urantia teaching is universalist in one sense. As noted, it reveals that *all* persons will resurrect after physical death. After a suitable orientation to the boundless opportunities of the universal plan for afterlife ascent, the average survivor chooses eternal life. This is the norm; in almost all circumstances, the Spirit slowly prevails over anyone who, having attained the first phase of the afterlife, possesses a flicker of willingness to yield to divine grace and forgiveness. Having "opted in," each willing person now progresses in an eternal life of ever-more-advanced moral, intellectual, social, and spiritual achievements. And whether this hope-filled narrative is true or not, the *UB*'s story of an eternal life of endless adventure is easily the most detailed elucidation of the afterlife in any scripture I know of.

We are told that this self-perfecting adventure of ascension to Paradise entails the traversal of several hundred stages of advancement. At some point in this afterlife journey we achieve "God-fusion" (irrevocable identification with the Indwelling Spirit), and eons later we attain actual perfection. In future ages, when the revelation of *UB* is (hopefully) more generally accepted, I believe its teaching about annihilation and the afterlife will be seen as one of its most significant contributions, with far-reaching implications for all Christian believers.

To conclude, I will simply quote a number of passages to emphasize the *UB*'s answer to this most important question in eschatology: "What happens if one chooses not to do the Father's will in some definitive way?"

Definition of annihilation. "When this sentence is finally confirmed, the sin-identified being instantly becomes as though he had not been. There is no resurrection from such a fate; it is everlasting and eternal. The living energy factors of identity are resolved by the transformations of time and the metamorphoses of space into the cosmic potentials whence they once emerged. As for the personality of the iniquitous ones, it is deprived of a continuing life vehicle by the creature's failure to make those choices and final decisions which would have assured eternal life" (2: 3.4).

Why annihilation? "God loves the sinner and *hates* the sin: such a statement is true philosophically, but God is a transcendent personality, and persons can only love and hate other persons. Sin is not a person. God loves the sinner because he is a personality reality (potentially eternal), while towards sin God strikes no personal attitude, for sin is not a spiritual reality; it is not personal; therefore does only the justice of God take cognizance of its existence. The love saves the sinner; the law of God destroys the sin. This attitude of the divine nature would apparently change if the sinner finally identified himself wholly with sin just as the same mortal mind may also fully identify itself with the indwelling spirit Adjuster. Such a sin-identified mortal would then become wholly unspiritual in nature (and therefore personally unreal) and would experience eventual incompleteness of being. Unreality, even incompleteness of creature nature, cannot exist forever in a progressively real and increasingly spiritual universe" (2: 6.8).

Every precaution taken. "Although conscious and wholehearted identification with evil (sin) is the equivalent of nonexistence (annihilation) there must always intervene between the time of such personal identification with sin and the execution of the penalty—the automatic result of such a willful embrace of evil—a period of time of sufficient length to allow for such an adjudication of such an individual's universe status as will prove entirely satisfactory to all related universe personalities, and which will be so fair and just as to win the approval of the sinner himself" (54:3.2).

Who judges? "The courts of the Ancients of Days (see glossary) are the high review tribunals for the spiritual adjudication of all competent universes. Mandates of judgment originate in the local universes, but sentences involving extinction of will creatures are always formulated on, and executed from, the headquarters of the superuniverse. The sons of the local universes can decree the survival of mortal man, but only the Ancients of Days may sit in executive judgment on the issues of eternal life and death" (15: 12.2). "… But if the question of the right of continued existence, life eternal, comes up for adjudication, it must be referred to the tribunals of Orvonton, and if decided adversely to the individual, all sentences of extinction are carried out upon the orders, and through the agencies, of the judges of the super-government" (33: 7.4).

Archangels as record keepers. "This enormous corps of recorders busy themselves with keeping straight the record of each mortal of time from the moment of birth up through the universe career until such an individual either leaves Salvington for the superuniverse regime or is 'blotted out of recorded existence' by the mandate of the Ancient of Days" (37:3.7).

God desires the salvation of all, "...for the Father himself loves you. It is in response to this paternal affection that God sends the marvelous Adjusters to indwell the minds of men. God's love is universal; 'whosoever will may come.' He would 'have all men be saved by coming into the knowledge of the truth.' He is 'not willing that any should perish'" (2:5.2).

Instruction for Teachers
and Believers

(The full text of Section 3, Paper 159, in *The Urantia Book*)

At Edrei, where Thomas and his associates labored, Jesus spent a day and a night and, in the course of the evening's discussion, gave expression to the principles which should guide those who preach truth, and which should activate all who teach the gospel of the kingdom. Summarized and restated in modern phraseology, Jesus taught:

Always respect the personality of man. Never should a righteous cause be promoted by force; spiritual victories can be won only by spiritual power. This injunction against the employment of material influences refers to psychic force as well as to physical force. Overpowering arguments and mental superiority are not to be employed to coerce men and women into the kingdom. Man's mind is not to be crushed by the mere weight of logic or overawed by shrewd eloquence. While emotion as a factor in human decisions cannot be wholly eliminated, it should not be directly appealed to in the teachings of those who would advance the cause of the kingdom. Make your appeals directly to the divine spirit that dwells within the minds of men. Do not appeal to fear, pity, or mere sentiment. In appealing to men, be fair; exercise self-control and exhibit due restraint; show proper respect for the personalities of your pupils. Remember that I have said: "Behold, I stand at the door and knock, and if any man will open, I will come in."

In bringing men into the kingdom, do not lessen or destroy their self-respect. While overmuch self-respect may destroy proper humility and end in pride, conceit, and arrogance, the loss of self-respect often ends in paralysis of the will. It is the purpose of this gospel to restore self-respect to those who have lost it and to restrain it in those who have it. Make not the mistake of only condemning the wrongs in the lives of your pupils; remember also to accord generous recognition for the most praiseworthy things in their lives. Forget not that I will stop at nothing to restore self-respect to those who have lost it, and who really desire to regain it.

Take care that you do not wound the self-respect of timid and fearful souls. Do not indulge in sarcasm at the expense of my simple-minded brethren. Be not cynical with my fear-ridden children. Idleness is destructive of self-respect; therefore, admonish your brethren ever to keep busy at their chosen tasks, and put forth every effort to secure work for those who find themselves without employment.

Never be guilty of such unworthy tactics as endeavoring to frighten men and women into the kingdom. A loving father does not frighten his children into yielding obedience to his just requirements.

Sometime the children of the kingdom will realize that strong feelings of emotion are not equivalent to the leadings of the divine spirit. To be strongly and strangely impressed to do something or to go to a certain place, does not necessarily mean that such impulses are the leadings of the indwelling spirit.

Forewarn all believers regarding the fringe of conflict which must be traversed by all who pass from the life as it is lived in the flesh to the higher life as it is lived in the spirit. To those who live quite wholly within either realm, there is little conflict or confusion, but all are doomed to experience more or less uncertainty during the times of transition between the two levels of living. In entering the kingdom, you cannot escape its responsibilities or avoid its obligations, but remember: The gospel yoke is easy and the burden of truth is light.

The world is filled with hungry souls who famish in the very presence of the bread of life; men die searching for the very God who lives within them. Men seek for the treasures of the kingdom with yearning hearts and weary feet when they are all within the immediate grasp of living faith. Faith is to religion what sails are to a ship; it is an addition of power, not an added burden of life. There is but one struggle for those who enter the kingdom, and that is to fight the good fight of faith. The believer has only one battle, and that is against doubt—unbelief.

In preaching the gospel of the kingdom, you are simply teaching friendship with God. And this fellowship will appeal alike to men and women in that both will find that which most truly satisfies their characteristic longings and ideals. Tell my children that I am not only tender of their feelings and patient with their frailties, but that I am also ruthless with sin and intolerant of iniquity. I am indeed meek and humble in the presence of my Father, but I am equally and relentlessly inexorable where there is deliberate evil-doing and sinful rebellion against the will of my Father in heaven.

You shall not portray your teacher as a man of sorrows. Future generations shall know also the radiance of our joy, the buoyance of our good will, and the inspiration of our good humor. We proclaim a message of good news which is infectious in its transforming power. Our religion is throbbing with new life and new meanings. Those who accept this teaching are filled with joy and in their hearts are constrained to rejoice evermore. Increasing happiness is always the experience of all who are certain about God.

Teach all believers to avoid leaning upon the insecure props of false sympathy. You cannot develop strong characters out of the indulgence of self-pity; honestly endeavor to avoid the deceptive influence of mere fellowship in misery. Extend sympathy to the brave and courageous while you withhold overmuch pity from those cowardly souls who only halfheartedly stand up before the trials of living. Offer not consolation to those who lie down before their troubles without a struggle. Sympathize not with your fellows merely that they may sympathize with you in return.

When my children once become self-conscious of the assurance of the divine presence, such a faith will expand the mind, ennoble the soul, reinforce the personality, augment the happiness, deepen the spirit perception, and enhance the power to love and be loved.

Teach all believers that those who enter the kingdom are not thereby rendered immune to the accidents of time or to the ordinary catastrophes of nature. Believing the gospel will not prevent getting into trouble, but it will insure that you shall be *unafraid* when trouble does overtake you. If you dare to believe in me and wholeheartedly proceed to follow after me, you shall most certainly by so doing enter upon the sure pathway to trouble. I do not promise to deliver you from the waters of adversity, but I do promise to go with you through all of them.

And much more did Jesus teach this group of believers before they made ready for the night's sleep. And they who heard these sayings treasured them in their hearts and did often recite them for the edification of the apostles and disciples who were not present when they were spoken.

Some Key Celestial Authors Identified in the *UB*

The Urantia revelation is said to be the product of a large and diverse corps of celestial authors. This brief section lists only a small representative selection of the numerous celestial beings who, we are told, are either sponsors or coauthors of the *Urantia Papers*. (See the glossary for definitions of many of the terms that follow.)

At the top of the angelology scale we find beings of direct origin from the Paradise Trinity known as the *Ancients of Days*, who preside over our own galaxy supercluster, *Orvonton*. They are the very oldest created beings residing in the evolving universes, and there are just twenty-one of them; every superuniverse has a governing trio of Ancients of Days who serve as its chief administrators. Orvonton is said to one of the seven great inhabited *superuniverses*—as explained in Appendix B and elsewhere herein. We learn that a wide array of celestial beings were commissioned—under the authority of the *Ancients of Days* of Orvonton—to be authors of specific Papers in Part I.

And among the very highest types of the celestial authors of Part III of the text are the *Solitary Messengers*. One member of this order is the author of Papers 107–112, which describe the personality, the Indwelling Spirit, and the evolving soul—the trio that constitutes selfhood according to the Urantia teaching. An entire Paper (23) is devoted to the work of these beings, who are of direct origin from the Infinite Spirit. They are described as the "personal corps" of the Third Person of the Trinity.

Roughly in the middle of the grand holarchy are beings called *Melchizedeks*, known on high as the chief educators of the universes. They are the authors of many of the more philosophically advanced materials in the text, including Papers 100–103. These Papers present the *UB*'s teaching on the psychology and philosophy of religion.

At the bottom of the angelology scale, as it were, are the *midwayers*—known by that name because they exist in an invisible domain *midway* between humans and lower angels such as *seraphim*. Midwayers are able to connect directly with us physically because of their close energetic proximity to the material realms. Many miracles having to do with direct auditory communication, instantaneous physical healing, and changes in the location of physical objects are quietly carried out by our midwayers cousins. Because they can draw nearest to us, they were the invisible interlocutors of the human group in Chicago who first received the Urantia Papers between the years of 1924 and 1945. A special commission of midwayers who followed Jesus closely during his lifetime were the authors of Part IV of the book, "The Life and Teachings of Jesus."

APPENDIX C

Urantia Cosmology and Contemporary Astrophysics

The celestial authors of the *UB* skillfully wove human sources into their revelations, but their efforts with regard to cosmology and the physical sciences must have been an exceedingly complex editorial challenge. Their general mandate required that they coordinate the very best existing human knowledge in these fields with a limited set of permitted revelations about the physical universe—while at the same time not over-revealing in such a way as to stymie scientific curiosity and discovery. The result is that the text offers its revelatory disclosures about the physical universe in the phraseology of the scientific discoveries accepted at the time the *UB* was authored (in the 1920s and 1930s), and yet it is also clear that these Papers go far beyond the cosmological paradigm of that generation of scientists. (The primary Papers concerning astrophysics and cosmology are 11, 12, 32, 41, and 42.)

With regard to astrophysics, the *UB*'s revelatory descriptions appear to match and possibly transcend much of today's human knowledge in this field some eight decades later, but these revelatory statements also appear alongside now-outdated information from a bygone era in the history of science. According to veteran *UB* student and amateur astronomer John Causland, "The book's astronomy is phrased in the language in use at the time. . . . [Yet] with some amazement, I began to see that the Urantia cosmology actually told a story suggestive of a physical universe that only now we're beginning to comprehend."

Causland and many other commentators suggest that the revelators must have timed their teachings to coincide with the work of astronomers such as Edwin Hubble, who was the first to discover the existence of galaxies outside the Milky Way. Causland speculates that before the *UB*'s celestial authors would have been permitted to reveal the size, structure, and age of our universe, our scientists would first have had to "earn" some rudimentary knowledge of the existence of far-flung galaxies and other large-scale formations outside of our own galaxy. Such discoveries were made possible by Hubble's first measurements, dating back to 1929, including his crucial discovery of the so-called red shift—which proves that the observable galaxies and all other structures are rapidly receding away from one another.

It would appear that the revelators had to utilize now outdated human sources around whose limited vision they could weave specific revelatory information, but many researchers state that they also provided confusing or ambiguous indications about this extragalactic universe of universes. In following their mandate to not reveal too much, they seem to have unnecessarily muddied the waters with quantitative data that is now known to be quite far off. The celestial authors also incorporated and blended several contradictory models of the universe extant in the early twentieth century. Further, they used terms such as "nebula," "galaxy," and "universe" almost interchangeably, as scientists did at that time; today these words have far more distinct meanings. Due to such complicating factors, the strictly physical cosmology of *The Urantia Book* is no longer reliable in a number of details.

For example, the Urantia text offers two apparently contradictory models of what constitutes a *superuniverse* (the most important large-scale unit of the inhabited evolutionary universe; see the glossary.). Some passages in the *UB* depict our superuniverse, named *Orvonton*, as coextensive with the Milky Way galaxy, while other statements strongly (and accurately) imply that Orvonton is of vastly greater size.

Many believe that our superuniverse simply cannot be a single galaxy that contains a trillion inhabited planets, as some interpreters of the *UB* believe. (As a reminder, the *UB* states that there are seven superuniverses, each containing about one trillion inhabited worlds.) Instead, Orvonton may be a designation for a massive clump of thousands of galaxies now known to be the Virgo Supercluster. The superclusters that today have been clearly identified by astronomers may well be the ultimate constituents of the evolving inhabited universe known in the *UB* as the *grand universe*. Our own Milky Way galaxy, which contains a mere billion inhabited worlds, is but a small unit of Orvonton.

Mother Spirit and Christ Michael: Local Universe Representatives of the Trinity

According to the Urantia revelation, *Christ Michael* is the Creator and Father of our local universe which, when fully evolved, will contain up to ten million inhabited planets. He is also known to us as the historical person Jesus Christ who incarnated here on *Urantia*— our planet Earth. We are told in the text that, in partnership with the *Mother Spirit* who is his deity equal, Christ Michael ministers from on high to each of us, his children on Earth. The reality of a "Father-Mother" deity partnership involving Christ is a new revelation to our world.

The divine affection of Michael and Mother for us is typified in the fact that Michael incarnated in the likeness of one of us; by their ongoing revelations of the "divine word" such as the *UB* itself; and by the ministrations to us of the vast angelic host created by Mother Spirit.

Somewhat similar to traditional Christianity, *The Urantia Book* offers a Trinitarian theology of Father, Son, and Spirit, but it updates these ancient concepts by providing unprecedented detail in the context of a modern scientific cosmology. The Eternal Trinity manifests in our local evolving universe through Christ Michael and Mother Spirit, who are deity partners in the mission of representing the Trinity in space-time. We are told that this divine pair perfectly depicts to our local universe the essence of the eternal deities that they represent.

Michael is said to be the direct and replete personalization of God the Father and the Eternal Son (the First and Second Persons of the Trinity) to this local universe. As explained in Paper 34:

> The Creator Sons of the Paradise order of Michael are the makers and rulers of the local universes of time and space. These universe

creators and sovereigns are of origin in the Father and Son but each is unique in nature and personality. Each is the "only begotten Son."

In addition, we are told in this Paper that the Infinite Spirit—the Third Person of the Trinity—*personalized* as the *Mother Spirit* for our segment of the universe. We also learn of our "encircuitment" through the Mother Spirit's *Holy Spirit* and through Christ Michael's *Spirit of Truth*.

A Mother Spirit does not and cannot incarnate in the flesh in the likeness of one of her human children, but Christ Michael possesses this singular function as a phase of his mercy ministry to inhabited planets. In his incarnation experiences he always manifests the infinite love and divine power of the Eternal Son. However, he is not the Eternal Son of the Trinity as asserted in Christian doctrine. He is in fact of origin from the Father *and* the Eternal Son.

In the final analysis, we can say that the founders of the Christian Church were correct about the spiritual relationships of the Trinity but never envisioned the complex factual reality of Trinity manifestations in the space-and-time universes that would be revealed centuries later in the *UB*.

Glossary

Adam and Eve

These unique divine beings serve as "reproducing couples" on inhabited evolutionary planets; a single pair known as "Adam and Eve" appears on each such world. They belong to the order of "Material Sons and Daughters of God" and reside on the system capitol (see "local system"). Our Adam-and-Eve pair materialized on Urantia nearly 38,000 years ago for the purpose of biologically uplifting the mortals of the realm, and for other important reasons. However, our planetary Adam and Eve faced an exceedingly difficult mission here compared to other planets, and ultimately defaulted. This occurred in part because of the planetary quarantine on Urantia, a result of the Lucifer Rebellion (see entry) that isolated them from routine contact with the larger universe. The garbled record of their story contained in Genesis is updated for the modern age in Papers 73-76 in *The Urantia Book*.

adjudication; adjudication of Lucifer Rebellion

The case of *Gabriel vs. Lucifer* was launched early in the twentieth century before the courts of the Ancients of Days (see entry); this event was concurrent with the reception of the Papers in Chicago that would later become *The Urantia Book*. An adjudication of this case would mean that the quarantine of Urantia is lifted so that all "off-world" communication circuits to the planet could be reinstated among many other changes. The reasons for the rebellion and the story of its aftermath are discussed at length in Papers 52 and 53. (See also the entry under "Lucifer Rebellion.")

Adjuster—see Thought Adjuster

Ancients of Days

In power, majesty, and scope of authority the Ancients of Days are the most versatile and mighty of the direct rulers of the time-space creations. They oversee the administration of *superuniverses* (i.e., galactic organizations that comprise approximately one trillion inhabited planets). In all of the vast evolutionary universe they alone are invested with the powers of final executive judgment concerning the eternal extinction of will creatures who have chosen not to survive in the afterlife after repeatedly rejecting all offers of mercy and rehabilitation. The Ancients of Days are the most perfect and the most divinely endowed rulers in all time-space existence. See Paper 18.

architectural spheres

These invisible worlds are purposely constructed for their intended uses in higher dimensions. The local universe of Nebadon (see entry) contains over 600,000 of these special spheres. While they may receive some light from nearby stars, these worlds are heated and lit independently and therefore do not emit enough light to be seen by Urantia's telescopes. Architectural worlds do not suffer from geologic instability or weather phenomena. They are made from morontia materials (see entry under "morontia"), and all architected worlds are said to be very beautiful. Each of us will see our first architectural sphere when we awaken from the death experience on mansion world number one. See especially Paper 15, sec. 7.

Avonal Son; Avonal order

The *Avonals* are high beings of the Avonal order, and they are one of three "descending" orders of beings of origin on Paradise (see entry); they also known as *Magisterial Sons* (see entry). "The Avonals are known as Magisterial Sons because they are the high magistrates of the realms, the adjudicators of the successive dispensations of the worlds of time. They preside over the awakening of the sleeping survivors, sit in judgment on the realm, bring to an end a dispensation of suspended justice, execute the mandates of an age of probationary mercy, reassign the space creatures of planetary ministry to the tasks of the new dispensation, and return to the headquarters of their local universe upon the completion of their mission." (20:3.1)

Christ Michael; Michael; Creator Son; Jesus Christ

Michael, or *Christ Michael,* is our local universe Father and Creator. He is also known to us as Jesus Christ, who incarnated as Jesus of Nazareth on our planet. He is of the order of *Michael,* high beings with creator prerogatives who are also known as *Creator Sons;* they are directly conceived by God the Father and God the Son and are thus of Paradise origin. In partnership with the Mother Spirits who are their deity equals (see "Mother Spirit"), Michaels create local universes and their myriad inhabitants, over which they rule with love and mercy. Their unending love for us is typified in the fact that they may incarnate in the likeness of their creatures on worlds they have created. See especially Papers 20 and 21 and also Appendix C.

central universe; Havona; billion worlds

The central universe is not a time creation; it is an eternal existence. This never-beginning, never-ending universe consists of one billion spheres of sublime perfection called *Havona,* and at its core is the stationary and absolutely stabilized *Isle of Paradise* (see "Paradise"). The mass of the central creation is far in excess of the total known mass of all seven sectors of the grand universe (the time-space creations). See especially Paper 14.

constellation; constellation level of authority

Constellations are comprised of one hundred local systems and consist of up to one-hundred thousand inhabited worlds. The name of our constellation's headquarters world is *Edentia,* and beings known as the *Most Highs* (see entry) preside there. See Paper 43.

cosmic mind

"The cosmic mind encompasses all finite-mind levels and co-ordinates experientially with the evolutionary-deity levels of the Supreme Mind and transcendentally with the existential levels of absolute mind." (42:10.6)

Eternal Son

The Eternal Son is the great mercy-minister to all creation. As the Second Person of the Trinity, he is known as the Original Son, and along with God the Father, he is the co-creator of other Paradise Sons (such as the *Michael* and *Avonal* orders, see entries). He is the source of spirit, the administrator of all spirit, and the center of spirit in the universe and therefore all things spiritual are drawn to him; he is co-eternal and co-ordinate with the Father, and is a full equal to the Father. "The Eternal Son is the perfect and final expression of the 'first' personal and absolute concept of the Universal Father. Accordingly, whenever and however the Father personally and absolutely expresses himself, he does so through his Eternal Son, who ever has been, now is and ever will be, the living and divine Word. The Eternal Son is the spiritual personalization of the Father's universal and infinite concept of divine reality, unqualified spirit, and absolute personality. As the Father is the First Great Source and Center, so the Eternal Son is the Second Great Source and Center." See Papers 6 and 7.

Fifth Epochal Revelation; epochal revelation

The purpose of revelation is to exalt and "up-step" the religions of evolution by periodic teachings tailored to the current needs and capacity for receptivity of the mortals of a given world. Every inhabited evolutionary planet receives a series of epochal revelations throughout its history. *The Urantia Book* is one example of such a gift, and is the fifth such epochal revelation to be given to Urantia. Among many other factors, the Fifth Epochal Revelation was designed to correct philosophical error, assess the evolutionary religions and sciences, and adjust planetary and human history to a factual account of events from the past.

fragment, Father Fragment—see Thought Adjuster

fusion

The makeup of our being, our true self, is a combination of the personality, the soul, and the divine Father Fragment within. The goal of our personal spiritual evolution is the eternal fusion of these elements;

in other words, these three aspects, when fused, are eternalized. For almost all of us on Earth today, fusion will only occur in our future heavenly life. Only a few documented cases of fusion exist while in a material body.

guardian angels; guardian seraphim; seraphim
Although many traditional teachings about guardian angels are mythic in nature, nevertheless they are real and play a crucial role in the spiritual destiny of mortals on all inhabited worlds. Their ministrations are always provided to individual humans. These seraphim generally serve in pairs and are assisted by *cherubim* and *sanobim*. In the beginning of a mortal's life, one seraphim pair will oversee a group of one thousand mortals with assistance from a company of cherubim; but as humans ascend in spiritual attainment, the numbers served by a seraphic pair become fewer in number, until such time as we achieve the requisite spiritual status to have a pair of destiny guardians assigned to us exclusively. Angels do not invade the human mind or interfere with the free will decisions of the mortals of their assignment, but they do subtly guide us into situations of learning and spiritual growth. At death, these "destiny guardians" become the custodial trustees of our life records, our identity specifications, and of our immortal souls, until we are repersonalized on the mansion worlds (see entry). They remain our companions for much of the time while we progress toward Paradise, simultaneously furthering their own advancement of seraphic education. See Paper 113.

God the Father; God; Father; Father-Mother; Paradise Father
As the universal Father (or Father-Mother), God is the First Source and Center of all things and beings. According to the Urantia revelation, the term "God" always denotes personality or personhood, but also infinitely more. God the Father is depicted as the infinite and eternal God of love, as well as Creator, Controller, and Upholder of the universe of all universes. The First Person of the Trinity—God the Father—loves us with an attitude analogous to that of a father; the love and mercy of God the Son, the Second Person of the Trinity, is akin to the love of a mother. *God the Spirit* is the Third Person of the

218 of Reason and Revelation

Trinity and is also known as *the Infinite Spirit*. See especially Papers 1 through 5.

Havona—see central universe

Light and Life; Age of Light and Life; Era of Light and Life
The goal of all inhabited planets, and the final evolutionary attainment of any world of time and space, is known as the *Age of Light and Life*. When a world has reached this utopian state of evolutionary consummation, its achievements along the way will have included the attainment of one worldwide language, one blended race, one unified world religion, universal peace, and a very advanced state of prosperity and happiness. See Paper 56.

local system
A local system consists of no more than one thousand inhabited or inhabitable worlds, and in the younger systems only a comparatively small number of these worlds may be inhabited. Each local system has an architectural sphere as its headquarters and is ruled by a *System Sovereign*. Our local system, named *Satania*, is not yet complete. So far there are 619 inhabited planets in the system. Urantia was the 606th world within the system to have life implanted on it. The administrative head of Satania is a *Lanonandek Son* named *Lanaforge*. He has served since shortly after Lucifer was deposed and incarcerated for disloyalty to the universe government. See Papers 45 and 46.

local universe; Nebadon
Our local universe, called *Nebadon*, was created by Christ Michael, and is ruled by Christ Michael and by our Mother Spirit (see entries). The local universe administrative headquarters is *Salvington*, which is also the heavenly abode of Michael and Mother. Nebadon is still in the process of formation (it will eventually contain 10,000,000 inhabited planets), and is one of 700,000 local universes within the Grand Universe. In Urantia Book cosmology, Paradise is a stationary body at the center of the space-time universe (see "central universe" and "Paradise"), which is surrounded by a universe of inherently perfect worlds

known as *Havona*, which is in turn encircled by seven discrete aggregations of galaxies (galaxy clusters) called *superuniverses*, each of which contains 100,000 local universes. See Papers 32 and 33.

Lucifer Rebellion

Lucifer was a high celestial being and the brilliant administrator of our local system of inhabited planets. Along with his first assistant named *Satan*, Lucifer launched a rebellion against the local universe government of Christ Michael some 200,000 years ago. Lucifer's insurrection created pandemonium on our planet and on 36 other worlds in our local system. Among his other contentions, Lucifer held that the Universal Father does not really exist, and he attacked the right of Christ Michael to assume sovereignty of Nebadon in the name of the Father. Tragically, the majority of celestial beings in the celestial hierarchy of our planet Urantia went over to the way of Lucifer, causing major distortions and destructive aberrations ever since. Some believe that the planet-wide era of conscious awakening known as the Correcting Time was launched in the mid-1980s after the final adjudication of the Lucifer rebellion in celestial courts. See Papers 53 and 54.

Magisterial Mission

A visitation by a *Paradise Son* of the *Avonal* order (see entries) occurs when a planet has reached an evolutionary limit of intellectual and ethical progress. These beings may also appear in judicial actions "at the end of an age" as so-called dispensation terminators. In this role they liberate sleeping survivors (those in repose after death) for resurrection in the mansion worlds of the afterlife. Each *Avonal Son* (also known as a *Magisterial Son*, see next entry) has at least one incarnating bestowal mission, where he is born of woman. On missions other than bestowals, they often appear in visible form as mature adult males. Planets may have numerous Magisterial Missions.

Magisterial Son; Avonal Son

These beings are the joint creation of the Eternal Son and the Infinite Spirit and thus are Paradise sons. There are about one billion in number in the grand universe, each one representing a new and divine ideal of loving service. They come into being as divine administrators, that is, as *descending Sons* who reveal themselves as servers, bestowers, judges, teachers, and truth revealers. They work closely with the Creator Sons, the Michaels, of each local universe. See Paper 20, sec. 1-4.

mansion worlds; mansonia
In the afterlife, those mortals who survive the transition of death are repersonalized on these architectural worlds; these seven heavenly planets are the first post-mortal residences for all survivors of life in the flesh. The mansion worlds are training worlds—the first two providing remedial training. Their chief purpose is to prepare us for the vast career ahead as we journey across the universe in our age-long ascent to God on Paradise. See Paper 47.

Michael Sons; order of Michael
This order of Paradise Son, some 700,000 in number, are created by a union of the Universal Father and the Eternal Son. Each one is known as the "only-begotten Son" because each is conceived as a unique individual personality. These Sons are, in effect, the personification of the Paradise Father-Son to and in their local universes. Each is destined to create a universe of his own making; and along with the Mother Spirit of that universe, they co-create the living beings that will inhabit this vast physical creation. Each Michael must earn the right to govern his local universe creation as its Sovereign, and does so by completing seven bestowals in which he incarnates as one of various order of beings that he himself co-created. In this way he becomes a wise, merciful, and loving brother and Father to his created sons and daughters. See Papers 21 and 33.

Michael; Christ Michael
The Creator of our local universe, Christ Michael, is Father and brother to all living beings of his creation, and is one and the same as Jesus Christ, who incarnated on Earth. He possesses and represents all the divine attributes and powers of the Eternal Son within the local universe of Nebadon, and has additional power and authority to fully represent the Universal Father to his creatures. To our local universe,

Christ Michael represents God; he is omnipotent, omniscient, and omnipresent. He is ably assisted by his consort, the Universe Mother Spirit. Their main concerns are creation, sustenance, and ministry; the two do not participate in judicial affairs because Creators never sit in judgment on their creatures. See UB, Paper 33.

morontia
In the local universe, the morontia realm is the vast reality domain intervening between the material and spirit levels of existence. We are told that "the warp of morontia is spiritual; its woof is physical." While material planets contain one hundred naturally occurring physical elements on their atomic chart (i.e., the periodic table of elements), the morontia realm has two hundred such elements. Morontia is a semi-material substance composed of varying mixtures of spirit and material energies. (Morontia substance is normally invisible to the human eye.) The human soul is comprised of this same material. With each step of progress through the morontia career in the afterlife, the ascender gradually becomes slightly less physical and slightly more spiritual, and each transition to a higher world necessitates a change of the body or life vehicle. See Paper 42, sec.10 and Paper 48, sec 1.

Most Highs; Most Highs of the constellation
Three so-called *Vorondadek Sons* rule over each constellation for a set period of years. The Most Highs are the invisible rulers of the polities or political organizations of humans on all planets and act as over-controllers of political evolution; they are occupied with groups, not individuals, and they foster the greatest good for the greatest number of people without violating human free will. One hundred local systems (see entry) or about 100,000 inhabitable planets make up a constellation. See Papers 43 and 134.

Mother Spirit; Universe Mother Spirit
Just as Michael is our local universe Father, the Mother Spirit is our local universe Mother. As Christ Michael is a personalization of the First and Second Persons of the Trinity, the Creative Mother Spirit is a personalization of the Third Person. She is Christ Michael's consort in

the administration and in the ministry of love and mercy to the myriad of planets in Nebadon (see entry). Among the many powers and duties of Mother Spirits is the ability to give life; she supplies the essential factor of living plasm to all creatures high and low. She also loves and ministers to us through her vast retinue of angels and other ministering celestial beings. See Paper 21.

Mystery Monitor—see Thought Adjuster

Nebadon; local universe
This is the name of the local universe in which our planet is located. Nebadon presently contains approximately 3,400,000 inhabited planets. It is a relatively young universe and sits on the outer edges of *Orvonton*, the superuniverse in which it is located. Nebadon is ruled by Christ Michael, also known as Jesus Christ, and his consort, the Mother Spirit, who are its Creators.

Paradise; Isle of Paradise; Paradise Sons
At the literal center of the cosmos—yet outside of space and time—is the only stationary body in all creation, and the Urantia revelation designates this stupendous reality as *Paradise*. God is personally present on Paradise; from his infinite being flow the floodstreams of life, energy, and personality to all universes. Paradise is an extremely large "island" located at "the geographical center of infinity." All physical and spiritual energies and all cosmic-force circuits, including all forms of gravity, have their origin at Paradise. It also has residential zones; all God-conscious mortals will someday attain and reside on Paradise. *Paradise Sons* are high beings of origin on Paradise. See Paper 11.

personality
This refers to that part of a person by which we know them as unique, and designates those personal qualities that endure and which are recognizable regardless of changes in age, status, behavior or other external qualities. We are told that personality is a very high and divine gift to each person from God the Father. It is that changeless meta-physical quality that confers upon them their unique identity in the

cosmos, and could be called the "image of God" within us. Personality is absolutely unique and immutable; it does not in itself evolve, but its relationship with the Indwelling Spirit (the Thought Adjuster) and the soul continually evolves. Functionally, personality also acts as the unifier and integrator of all aspects of an individual's relationship with himself/herself and with his or her environment.

Planetary Prince
A Planetary Prince appears on a world when it has evolved primitive human beings of "will status." Although a Planetary Prince is invisible to humans, his staff is visible. The staff sets up schools and teaches a variety of skills, such as cultivation of the soil, home building, and basic spiritual culture. The classes are progressive in nature; the mortals are taught agriculture, food preservation, government, sanitation, pottery, metal working and so on. The students are then sent out among their people to share the knowledge. The Prince and his staff normally stay on a world, teaching ever-higher concepts of wisdom, philosophy, brotherhood and religion, until a planet reaches the Age of Light and Life. Urantia's Prince *Caligastia* served admirably for 300,000 years before following his superior, Lucifer, into rebellion, about 200,000 years agao. Caligastia was then removed from his post. (See Lucifer Rebellion.) See Paper 66.

quarantine; quarantined worlds
Worlds and systems that have participated in open rebellion or disloyalty to the Creator Son are placed in isolation until the courts of the Ancients of Days (see entry) are able to rule on the matter. Urantia and 36 other inhabited worlds were placed in quarantine (all communications severed) when Lucifer and Caligastia went into rebellion against the universe government.

seraphim (see also *guardian angels*)
The order of seraphim are the angels we have come to know in literature and scripture, and they always come in pairs (but are not winged). A large category of beings created by the local universe Mother Spirit,

they serve in a myriad of ways. There are over five hundred million pairs of seraphim on our planet. See Papers 26, 30, 31, 37–40.

soul

The Indwelling Spirit or Thought Adjuster is a perfect gift of God, but the soul is an experiential human achievement. When we choose the divine will and live in accord with it, or when we follow the path of higher values such as truth, beauty, and goodness, the invisible effect is that our soul grows in substance and quality. We are told in *The Urantia Book* that the Indwelling Spirit is the *father* of our soul, just as the material mind (as the seat of moral choice) is the *mother* of the emerging soul. In the afterlife, the soul survives death and becomes the container of our actual identity through the agency of our personality and with the assistance of our guardian seraphim and other beings. See Paper 111.

Spirit of Truth

This is the unique and powerful spiritual endowment conferred on each person as a gift from our Creator Son, Christ Michael. This high and pure spiritual influence was gifted universally to all of humankind on the day of Pentecost. The Spirit of Truth enhances each person's ability to recognize truth. Its effectiveness is limited by each person's free-will consecration of his or her will to doing the will of God. When actively sought, the Spirit of Truth purifies the human heart and leads the individual to formulate a life purpose based on the love of truth.

Supreme Being; God the Supreme; the Supreme

The Supreme Being is the evolving deity of time and space. This deity is not a direct creator, but rather is the synthetic co-ordinator of all creature-Creator (or "co-creative") universe activities. The Supreme Being, now actualizing in the evolutionary universes, is the Deity correlator and synthesizer of time-space divinity, the ultimate summation of the value-laden import of all personal experience of all creatures on all worlds. The Supreme is the "world-soul" and the repository of the universal *akashic field* always being created by evolving souls everywhere. See Paper 115.

Thought Adjuster; Indwelling Spirit; Father Fragment; Mystery Monitor; Adjuster
This is the specialized term for "God-within"—the indwelling spark of God; we are told that an actual "fragment" of God the Father indwells every normal-minded and morally conscious human being. The TA is wholly subservient to our will, yet represents the actual will of God literally resident in our own minds. Through the practice of stillness, meditative worship, deep contemplation, genuine prayer, and loving service to others, we can attune ourselves to the influence of this inner divinity, thereby discerning the will of God for us as individuals. Also known as the Father Fragment or Mystery Monitor, the Adjuster is God's gift to each of us in addition to our personality, and its influence arouses our hunger for perfection, our quest for the divine. In addition, our Thought Adjuster and our material mind, working together, actually create our soul (see "soul"). According to *The Urantia Book*, the great goal of our spiritual evolution is to actually fuse with the Adjuster—i.e., come into complete union and identification with this Indwelling Spirit of God, and by so doing achieve immortality. See Papers 107 and 108.

Trinity; Paradise Trinity
This term refers to the eternal deity union of the Universal Father, the Eternal Son, and the Infinite Spirit. See Paper 10.

Urantia ("you-ran-sha")
Urantia is the name by which our planet is known in our local universe, according to the celestial authors of *The Urantia Book*. Urantia is said to be a backward and disturbed planet by virtue of its participation in the Lucifer Rebellion, and yet is a very blessed world because it was the site of the incarnation bestowal of Michael as Jesus of Nazareth.